Catahoula Leo]

Catahoula Leopard Dog Training Book Includes: Catahoula Leopard Dog Socializing, Housetraining, Obedience Training, Behavioral Training, Cues & Commands and More

Copyright © 2015

Acknowledgements

I would like to express my gratitude to the many people who saw me through this book; to all those who provided support, talked things over, offered comments and assisted in the editing, proofreading and design.

I would like to thank my publisher for enabling me to publish this book. Above all I want to thank my family, who supported and encouraged me through this journey.

Last but not least, I would like to thank all the Catahoula Leopard Dog lovers out there that helped inspire me to write this book. You are all a great inspiration.

Thank You.

Table of Contents

Chapter One: Introduction

The mutualistic symbiotic relationship between humans and dogs has been found to extend back for more than 30,000 years. Perhaps continuing research will push this date back even further – speculation based on findings in caves has placed a date of up to 300,000 years ago on the beginning of the dog/human partnership. Our relationship with dogs has proved to be beneficial for both species on several levels, including the emotional, which demonstrates that our dependence upon one another goes past a mere physical need.

It is quite easy to imagine how our relationship with dogs began, when humans were living around so many large and dangerous beasts. During the Paleolithic era, when most scientists agree that we and dogs got together, humans not only had to contend with large, dangerous herbivores like mammoths, wooly rhinoceros, and aurochs, but also with animals that preyed directly on them such as cave lions, wolves, and cave bears. Dogs would have provided not only some protection against these predators, especially in union with their humans, but also as an early warning system.

Flying in the face of conventional thinking is the possibility that our domestic dogs did not evolve from wolves. However, there are some very convincing arguments to be made that dogs developed from a now extinct canine form. Wolves can be considered to be impossible to truly tame or train. During the Middle Ages, a concerted effort was made by the hunting nobility in Europe to domesticate the wolf since it was stronger and hardier than any of the dogs, even mastiffs, that were used for hunting big game. The effort was a total failure; basically, although wolf puppies will seem to tame and become attached to humans, once they reach sexual maturity, they revert to a wild 'frame of mind'. The same happens with nearly every other wild animal that humans have raised; once the animal reaches puberty it becomes unreliable. Male wolves kept in a captive state, even if familiar with the keeper, will attack the keeper if he or she comes between him and a female in estrus.

Our ancestors, dealing with challenging environmental conditions, would not have had much to do with a large predator like the wolf, which preyed on human beings. Humans of the time would have seen the wolf as a competitor or threat.

Wolves still attack and even kill human beings today, after centuries of decimation of the animals has left the most timid wolves in the gene pool. How much bolder, and more ferocious those early wolves must have been – humans have never domesticated tigers for much the same reasons; the animals are powerful killers, not animals content to beg for scraps from raggle-taggle early humans. It may be much more likely that a smallish, now extinct dog that came slinking to a campfire for scraps, rolling onto its back to present its belly, is a much more likely candidate for domestication than the ferocious wolf. These smaller canids would have to have shown themselves to be amenable to training fairly quickly, otherwise they probably would have ended up being roasted on a spit.

The Fox Experiment

A very interesting experiment was conducted by Dmitry Belyaev, who was a Soviet geneticist. Using silver foxes, Belyaev instituted a breeding program that was supposed to show how selective breeding could turn a wild animal, such as a wolf, into a domestic dog. Over a span of 40+ years, Belyaev and his assistants chose the most amenable and least fearful kits from litters of silver foxes and bred them together. At the time of Belyaev's death in 1985, the experiment had only progressed for 26 years, and has continued until recently. As time passed, the researchers found that both the physical and mental characteristics of the foxes changed – they started barking, they showed variation in size, and their coat color, length, and texture changed. The ears of the foxes became floppy. Most significantly, a proportion of the former foxes sought the company of humans, wagging their tails and whining to attract attention.

Chapter One: Introduction

While this monumental study, which actually used something like 35,000 foxes over the course of the experiment, does show that it is possible to transform semi-tame foxes from fur farms into dogs, it also illustrates something else – the sheer impossibility of early humans, struggling to survive in a hostile and incredibly dangerous world, to manipulate by selective breeding a vicious and unpredictable predator like the wolf to become their tame and friendly companions. How on earth could people who lived on the edge of starvation and predation themselves, often in a nomadic lifestyle as they followed the herds on their migrations, have devoted the time and energy and foresight needed to transform wolves into dogs. Doesn't it make more sense to suppose that dogs something like the pariah dogs of today are the ancestors of the dogs that share our lives currently? The sheer logistics of the fox project, which even began with semi-tame foxes, would certainly be beyond the scope of Cro-Magnon, or Early Modern Human, mankind.

DNA studies are often touted as 'proving' that dogs evolved from wolves, but actually prove little more than that over the eons some dogs have been bred to wolves. Huskies and sled dogs are routinely bred to wolves from time to time to increase their hardihood, while the so-called 'timber shepherds' are hybrids resulting from crossing a German Shepherd (usually), with a wolf. Keep in mind that DNA testing is not the most exact science; in most testing procedures, the DNA from two animals, say a wolf and a German Shepherd, is mixed together, then allowed to settle out. The degree of relatedness is then determined by how many pieces of the wolf chromosome come together with the German Shepherd chromosome. This probably works in a general way. Keep in mind, too, that the Pekingese is thought to be one of the dogs closest to the wolf, something which the morphology of the Pekingese screams against.

Divorcing wolves from dogs is important as far as dog training is concerned because many theories about dog behavior and training are based on the social structure of a wolf pack. It would perhaps be better to examine the behavior of pariah dogs or feral dogs to get a closer approximation of the behavior of the real ancestors of today's dogs.

Pack Behavior in Wild and Feral Canids

Undoubtedly, the behavior of wolves in a wild state has been one of the most studied. Researchers have, up until fairly recently, considered that wolf packs were groups of perhaps partially-related and non-related individuals kept in line by an 'alpha' male and female. Studies of wild wolves have shown that wolf 'packs' are actually family groups, with the parent wolves being, of course, the leaders, and the younger wolves their variously aged offspring. Most wolf packs only contain 5 to 7 members, although pack size is in direct proportion to the availability of prey animals.

The younger wolves eventually leave the pack when they are 2 to 3 years old to find mates with which to begin their own family group, but before they branch off, they do help to care for their younger siblings as well as participating in hunts. There is dominance behavior shown to the younger family members by the parents, but constant jockeying for the top position is not part of the family structure.

African hunting dogs show some similarities with wolf family groups, but there are some important differences. While African hunting dog social structure is based generally on a family group, these groups are usually larger than that displayed by wolves, and groups will often combine when herbivores are migrating to take advantage of the large amount of prey. As with wolves, hunting dogs have only one breeding pair in the group, but it seems that males in the group can move up to occupy the top position by fighting. Older, displaced males are usually allowed to remain in the pack. Only the younger female hunting dogs leave the pack to join other groups – male offspring or 'adoptees' do not.

Jackals and coyotes show very similar breeding and social behavior in their respective niches. In both cases, as is that with wolves, young of these species stay with the parents for several years before leaving to establish their own families. During this time, they help with care of the new young and learn the refinements of hunting and scavenging.

And, although most people think of foxes as being entirely solitary animals except for the mother and her kits, this species does exhibit a family structure very much like that of other wild canids. The parent foxes establish a hunting territory, like wolves, coyotes, and jackals, and use this as a base in which to raise their young. The young from the previous year often do remain with the parents for a time to assist with raising the new litter. If the chances seem good, it is likely that non-breeding individuals will leave to establish their own territories, but the young will stay with the parents for an extended period should there be little opportunity for them.

The family, or pack, structure of all of the above animals is very similar, and another similarity they have is that the dominant pair is monogamous. This differs greatly from the social life that is observed in pariah (feral) dogs. Pariah dogs do not form family packs at all; dogs that are unattached to humans follow the same pattern around the world – they may come together briefly to exploit a food resource, or when a female is in heat, but there is no cohesive structure, and the 'pack' evaporates as soon as the control is removed. Feral female dogs will mate with any number of males, unlike the wild canids where the female mates with only one male dog.

In another respect, feral dogs show none of the family structure present in wolves, jackals, or foxes. The mother dog has sole responsibility for raising the litter of pups – the father takes no part. Young dogs soon leave their mothers to live a semi-solitary existence. Feral dogs will 'hang around' in the same general area, but have yet to show any real tendency to fight for an alpha position.

There is another interesting side to the supposition that dogs evolved from wolves, and that is that when once domesticated animals become feral, after several generations they revert to the original type. In other words, if a flock of chickens escaped confinement and were able to survive and breed away from human intervention, they would come to more closely resemble the red jungle fowl which is their distant ancestor. With regards to dogs that become separated from active association with humans, feral dogs revert to the basic pariah dog model – they do not become wolves.

Training Theories Based on Pack Behavior

A great many of today's dog training strategies are based on early observations of a captive wolf pack. These were wolves that were basically thrown indiscriminately together in a zoo in Switzerland. Unlike natural wolf packs, based on family structure and hierarchy, these wolves were strangers to one another, and denied of any opportunity to disperse, had little alternative than to fight with one another. In a wolf family, there is a dominance hierarchy, with the father and mother wolves at the top; it's only natural that even in an artificial situation, the instinctive drive for a normal 'pack' structure would surface, although in a completely distorted manner.

Most dog training programs have been based on these early, flawed descriptions of wolf pack behavior. These training programs generally call for the dog owner to exert his or her authority over the dog at all times, but especially when training the animal. Letting your dog walk in front of you or eat before you do were thought to undermine your authority as the pack leader. These theories do have some basis in reality if the wolf pack model is followed – the parent wolves do maintain their authority over the younger wolves, and will discipline them if their behavior violates the established behavior. Adult wolves will attack their older offspring for attempting to mate with one another or with the parents. Tempers appear to become shorter the closer it comes to the time when the young wolves would normally leave the family group.

It seems very probable, that if one accepts at least the possibility that domestic dogs evolved from a small to medium scavenging canine that hung around humans, that the wolf pack model is wrong to either a greater or lesser extent. Humans and dogs have interacted for so many thousands of years, and have developed so many intricacies of behavior with one another that training based strictly on forming dominance over the dog is probably incorrect. Experiments with tame wolves and dogs have shown over and over that dogs will turn to their humans for help when presented with a task beyond their means, whereas the wolves will struggle on (to reach food, for instance) even if there is no way for them to attain their goal by themselves.

Yes, obviously dogs must be subordinate to the humans, but the object of training should never be to break the dog's spirit, but to help the dog form a stronger relationship with the human family, one that is based more on trust and respect than aggression and fear.

Why Training Works – Human/Dog Mutualism

There are considered to be three symbiotic relationships in nature: parasitism, commensalism, and mutualism. Parasitism is well understood by nearly everyone and involves one species benefitting at the expense of another; internal parasites such as roundworms or liver flukes come to mind, as well as external parasites such as ticks and fleas. Commensalism is a symbiotic condition where one of the partners will benefit, and while the other receives no harm, it likewise receives no benefit; air plants (epiphytes) such as orchids and bromeliads, attach themselves to the trunks and limbs of trees, lessening the chances of predation by plant eaters and exposing them to more sunlight than they would have received on the forest floor, and cattle egret follow herds of cattle to eat the insects that the cattle inadvertently disturb – in both of these cases, the host tree or the cow receives no benefit, but neither is it hurt in any way.

The relationship between dogs and humans, however, is probably one of the best examples of mutualism. Over the thousands of years of our association with dogs, our mutual dependence upon the other species has actually changed both physiologically as well as psychologically. Humans and dogs have grown so close that our genes have come to mirror each other in certain important areas: digestion, brain functions, diet, and diseases. In fact, some researchers have conducted tests to demonstrate that the reactions of dogs to different stimuli create identical brain waves to those produced by human beings. Dogs are the only animals that look at both sides of our faces when interacting with us, and they learn to smile by watching us; they are intelligent enough to pick up on the emotions that accompany smiling and use their smiles appropriately.

Dogs have been found, by using brain scans, to share the same set of emotions that their owners do. These were things that those who are close to dogs knew already, but now science has proven this. The areas of the brain dealing with emotions such as joy, love, or jealousy match those of humans, and dogs react in the same way, with the same brain waves, as do their owners when these emotions are stimulated. Dogs are considered to have the intelligence of a human toddler, and it is only their inability to actually speak that stands in the way of what might be considered a more perfect bonding with humans.

However, it is precisely this mutualistic relationship that lends itself so well to training dogs. Not only are dogs highly intelligent, they also 'think' like we do. Over the course of human/dog evolution, dogs have been shaped to fulfill different needs – hunting, guarding, active protection, herding, and simply as companions. The trainability of dogs depends not only on their breed, but also upon the individual. Dogs of a certain breed, gun dogs or herding dogs, for example, are generally easy to train as they have worked in tandem with their owners to achieve a certain goal.

In my experience, Catahoulas are not the most difficult of dogs to train, however a key determining factor in successful training lies within the individual owner's experience and variations of applied approach.

Guard dogs tend to be more independent minded as they evolved to provide guarding for flocks or even villages without humans being present at all times. Some were expected to be able to make decisions on their own, and while this was obviously a useful trait while guarding a flock of sheep in an isolated situation on the Central Anatolian Plateau, it can cause training difficulties. However, always keep in mind that most problems concerning training can be overcome by using the correct technique and approach.

Training your Catahoula requires patience, technique, and an understanding and acceptance of the characteristics of your dog's breed. Properly training your dog will not only help to establish the dog's position in the family, but will help to establish a stronger bond between owner and pet.

Chapter Two: Socializing Your Catahoula

The need for active socialization will vary from breed to breed, depending on breed characteristics, but even a good-natured companion dog like a Catahoula will benefit from being socialized. Unless the breeder from whom you purchase your Catahoula has taken an extremely active part in raising your puppy, you may find that your new Catahoula is a bit shy and perhaps apprehensive around people and other pets. This may be perfectly normal, but a Catahoula who is never socialized will probably never be the confident and self-assured dog it should be.

Years ago, when I helped to raise a litter of puppies, I made it a point to handle them every day, right from birth. Because the mother was incapable of caring for them, I cleaned them and helped them feed, even providing supplemental feedings when one of them started to lose weight. Now, even though they were used to my smell and the touch of my hands, when their eyes opened, and they saw how huge I was in comparison, they were actually afraid of me. I was able to overcome this fairly quickly, but imagine how a puppy who has never had this kind of treatment must feel when they first enter a new home – it must be very frightening to them. My puppies had no problems whatsoever with meeting new people and all of them adjusted to their new homes without any problem at all; basically, they came pre-socialized in a way.

However, you should keep something in mind before you take your Catahoula puppy around to different situations to help socialize it – your pup should have had its required vaccinations. Many canine diseases are easily transmittable (such as distemper, parvovirus, and coronavirus) and are usually more serious in young dogs than they will be in older ones. Puppies do receive some immunity from their mother's milk, but this will wear off quickly and leave your Catahoula exposed to various bacterial and viral diseases.

The first dogs your Catahoula should meet should be those of friends or relatives that are calm and friendly animals. Don't hesitate to ask whether the dogs have been vaccinated themselves, as inoculations are not 100% effective. You can even arrange to have your Catahoula puppy meet the other dogs on 'neutral ground', such as during a walk. Stay positive and praise your pup when it responds favorably to the meeting.

Catahoulas, like all dogs, have psychological windows during which receptivity to new experiences will be most likely to be positive. When your Catahoula puppy is around 12 to 14 weeks old, this is the perfect age to begin socialization. Once again, pay attention to vaccinations before embarking on this. This is also the perfect time for you to begin using very mild forms of discipline with your puppy. By mild forms of discipline, I mean telling the puppy "No" in a fairly stern voice. It does **not** mean striking the puppy in any way or confining it to a crate to punish it. Relying mostly on positive reinforcement with occasional verbal reprimands will actually make your pup more confident because it will realize that it can depend on you to take care of it. Even a Catahoula will try to move to the dominant position in a home if there seems to be no leadership available, but dogs seem to understand that they are not really competent to act as the alpha in the household and will actually appreciate it when you show yourself to be the leader. You, your family, and your Catahoula will be all the happier if you attend to this facet of socialization.

Besides allowing your Catahoula to meet other dogs and people, it's a good idea to take it to different situations such as parks, streets in towns or cities, other people's homes, stores that may allow dogs inside, etc. This allows your Catahoula puppy to become accustomed to noise and movement, so it will be less likely to be fearful or panic in the future.

Always remember to keep your Catahoula on a leash when outside the home. Some owners choose to use a harness instead of a collar. You may find that a harness is better for control. It will also be more comfortable for your Catahoula since no pressure will be placed on the throat.

Enrolling your Catahoula puppy in puppy obedience classes is also a good way to socialize it. Not only will it allow your pup to interact with other young dogs and their owners, but it will help with discipline in a positive manner. Catahoulas that have exhibited shyness can often get over it by attending puppy obedience classes. Not only will your Catahoula learn how to behave, but you will also be taught how to effectively train your pup. Make certain the operator of the class has certification and experience, and it's best to speak to them beforehand to get an idea of their methods. If you have no idea where to find a puppy obedience class, ask your veterinarian for a recommendation.

Chapter Three: Housetraining Catahoula Puppies and Adults

Using the house or apartment as a bathroom is probably one of the greatest reasons, other than aggression, why dogs wind up in animal shelters. Housetraining is often looked upon as being one of the major hurdles that a Catahoula puppy or dog must overcome before being completely accepted as a member of the family. The time and effort that it takes to housetrain a puppy, or even an adult, can be extensive, so patience, as well as consistency, is required. If you react with anger, screaming, and striking the animal, it will only have a negative effect and can cause long-term psychological problems with your pet, as well as not advancing the project one jot.

In most cases, Catahoula puppies will be acquired from a kennel. Kennels handle the housing of dogs much differently than ordinary pet owners who might occasionally produce a litter of pups. Dogs in kennels, and litters of pups, are kept in fairly small enclosures, sometimes with no opportunity to go outside at all. One of the adult dogs we got from a kennel had never been out of her cage at all, and she actually had trouble walking; she would trip over a twig on the ground, literally. Slowly, she learned how to walk normally and run, and did she love to stretch out her length once she figured out how to do it, it was pure joy for her. These animals never have the opportunity to learn how to use the outdoors for elimination, and must use their living space when they urinate or defecate. Catahoula puppies from kennels or puppy mills, and adult dogs adopted from them, are starting at ground zero in regards to housetraining, and must be taught the proper elimination behavior.

Interestingly, when we had a litter of Catahoula puppies years ago, they were given the run of the house along with their parents. To begin with, of course, they simply went to the bathroom wherever the urge took them, and we just cleaned the messes up without comment. However, they observed their mother and father going outside to do their business, and at 6 weeks, one of the puppies started going to the door, asking to go out; it was truly an incredible sight to see that tiny puppy standing at the door, waiting to be let outside. We also worked with all the puppies to at least begin housetraining. When these 4 pups were adopted by other people, none of them eliminated in their new homes even once, not even to mark territory; all of them instantly went outside, even using doggy doors after being shown. From this, it's hard to escape the conclusion that even very young puppies are capable of being housetrained fairly easily as long as they have the example of older dogs and a little help from their human friends.

When we brought our last Catahoula puppies home, we allowed them to sleep in our bed right from the start. They spent their first night snuggled next to us. There was no whining or crying, and they settled down and went to sleep without a fuss. They got up once during the night to urinate, and never soiled the bed either.

We humans should keep in mind that up until the time that puppies join their new family, they are accustomed to sleeping with their mother and siblings; they are warm and in constant physical contact with others, which makes them feel secure, and we mirrored this as much as possible with our pups. Within 2 weeks these 3 month old puppies were sleeping through the night, and they still maintain this schedule after 11 years.

Unrealistic Expectations

Obviously, there are very few people who appreciate finding their rug soaked with urine or dog feces on the floor. And, unfortunately, many people react with anger when they find an unwanted 'deposit'. Housetraining takes a great deal of work, especially with Catahoula puppies, and if you're looking for a 5 day miracle, you are going to be sadly disappointed. Thinking that you can housetrain a puppy in under a week is analogous to thinking that a human child of 8 months can be taken out of diapers – it just can't be done.

Chapter Three: Housetraining Catahoula Puppies and Adults

Housetraining a puppy will require weeks of fairly intensive interaction with the pup, and this can be especially difficult if the pup will be left alone for long hours while you are at work. It is, naturally, easiest to housetrain your pet if you are there throughout the day to monitor the pup, but it can be achieved even if you are out of the home during the day.

You will become far less frustrated and irritated if you take the whole process slowly and methodically, and keep a fairly philosophical outlook such as 'this too shall pass'. Puppies and dogs don't want to soil their home, and are not doing this to get back at you in any way.

There are a series of dog breeds that appear to have their own schedule in regards to housetraining with some breeds being much easier to train than others. There are, however, plenty of breeds that may present more of a housebreaking challenge to the owner.

Smaller dogs in general are considered to be more difficult to housetrain than larger dogs, and owners of such should be prepared to be patient with their dog. The most difficult pup or adult dog to housebreak will nearly always be trained if enough time and patience is invested in the project. As far as housetraining goes, there is absolutely no place for negative reinforcement in the process. Praise should be used for success, and failures should be completely ignored.

With your Catahoula, be sure to display absolute patience at every step of the process. Catahoulas, like most dogs, are very sensitive to the reactions of their owners.

Starting Sensibly with Your Catahoula Puppy

The first thing to understand is that the gastrointestinal system and urinary system are still in a developmental stage in a puppy that is only a couple of months old. When puppies are born, they require the assistance of the mother to go to the bathroom, she licks their bottoms to stimulate them to urinate and defecate. This is obviously a strategy to keep the den clean. Once they start moving about a bit on their own, pups will still have no ability to hold urine or feces for some weeks to come and will soil indiscriminately; their mother still cleans up after them at this point.

Consider that a Catahoula puppy younger than 12 weeks will be unable to control its bowel and bladder functions, you may luck out like we did with our 6 week old puppy, but in most cases, you will be dealing with a puppy that has no idea of where to eliminate. There are several reasons why this occurs, and it should never be considered that the puppy is being disobedient:

Chapter Three: Housetraining Catahoula Puppies and Adults

1. The bladder of a puppy, especially of the smaller breeds, is relatively tiny. As time goes on, it will stretch out and expand, but initially it is little more than a tube. There would be no way that a puppy could 'hold it' at this early point.

2. The sphincter muscles of the bladder and colon are not developed in a very young dog so are unable to exert any control.

3. In order for a puppy to be able to control itself, the neural connections between the brain, bladder, and colon must be completed, and this will proceed as nature has provided; there is no way that this can be hurried along.

Expecting too much from your Catahoula puppy to begin with is a perfect recipe for frustration and anger on your part and fear on that of the puppy. Results will occur much more quickly and reliably when the owner is patient and avoids negativity of any kind.

Probably the most important facet of housetraining is to get the puppy onto a schedule as quickly as possible. You should feed the puppy at the same times every day, and the pup should go to bed at the same time every night. Establishing a routine is essential for helping your puppy learn how and when to use papers or the outdoors for elimination. You can start this as soon as you get your puppy, even if it is too young to actually be housetrained. This is also a good way just to help the pup feel more confident in regards to the new family and situation.

Take the puppy out every hour during the day, if possible, to help establish this as a routine too. You will be able to gradually lengthen the time between trips as the puppy gets older. Either forego outside trips or make them very brief if the weather is beastly, as this can act as an unintentional negative reinforcement too. Short-haired puppies will be very uncomfortable during cold or rainy weather and will often resist going outside because of this; sometimes a coat or sweater can help.

However you start housetraining your puppy, never, ever yell at your puppy, strike it, or rub its nose in the mess. Even telling the pup "No!" in a loud voice is totally unnecessary, this is not a discipline problem, it is a biological barrier to be overcome. Not only is this only providing negative reinforcement, some of these reactions are cruel and will only serve to make your pup afraid of you.

Paper Training

There are a number of reasons why you may want to start housetraining your Catahoula puppy with paper training: you live in an apartment and getting the puppy outside quickly could be difficult, the winter weather is so extreme that you hesitate to expose a very young puppy to it, and you are not present in the home during part of the day. The point of paper training is to get the puppy used to going to the bathroom in one or two spots, rather than anywhere the urge takes the pup. This will probably require quite a few newspapers, so it's a good idea to start stocking up before you even bring your puppy home. Some people prefer to use 'training pads' for this rather than newspaper, and these do have the advantage of having plastic on the bottom to prevent leakage.

Simply expect your new puppy to urinate and defecate on the floor, and this is actually the first step to paper training. You should just take this in stride; don't make any kind of fuss over this, either positive or negative. Your puppy will naturally be attracted to where urine or feces have been previously, so use some of these substances to train your puppy.

1. Place the paper you will be using near your exit or exits if possible, this will help the puppy to learn to associate elimination with going outside in time. One of our females still goes over to one of the places where she was taught to use newspapers when she was a puppy as a signal that she wants to go out.

2. When your Catahoula pup squats or hunches up on the floor, say nothing, but take a bit of the mess and put it on the paper. You don't need much, just enough to provide the scent of the urine or feces for the newspapers or training pads.

3. Take the puppy over to the paper and let it smell what's on it. You can usually remove the bait as soon as the puppy has smelled it; enough of the scent will remain to act as an attractant.

4. Repeating this several times will usually be enough to get your puppy to make the connection between going to the bathroom and using the paper, or training pad.

5. Be sure to pile on the praise as soon as your puppy uses the paper by itself. Don't let the papers get too dirty, though, pick up feces immediately and change the paper once the pup has used it for urination several times. If it gets too stinky, the puppy will avoid the spot.

6. You can start moving the paper closer to the outside as soon as the puppy uses it reliably, and most pups will soon catch on that they can use the yard as easily as they can their paper. Be sure to allow additional time for your Catahoula to be reliably housetrained.

7. As with paper training, use some urine-soaked paper and a bit of feces in your yard where you want the pup to go,

and this will be the place they will usually use. Be sure to pick up feces from the yard quickly; dogs don't like to go to the bathroom in a dirty place, and stepping in dog feces is singularly unpleasant.

In our experience with Catahoula puppies, it only took a few times before they used the papers without fail. We were in the middle of a severe northern winter when we got them and didn't want to expose them to the cold while they were so young, and had little hair, so we actually let them use the papers longer than we ordinarily would have. As soon as the weather became warmer, they started using the yard without any problem, and none of them had any accidents in the house thereafter.

The 'Grab and Run' Technique

This technique can work quite well as long as you are in the home constantly. It will also depend not only on sticking to a tight schedule, but also on nearly continual observation of the puppy. As with the paper training method, it's important to establish a schedule the puppy can rely upon. Feeding the Catahoula at the same times every day will start to regularize the puppy's digestive system. For a very young dog, always keep in mind that their digestion works on the principle of 'in one end, and out the other'.

Chapter Three: Housetraining Catahoula Puppies and Adults

1. As soon as the puppy has had a meal, or has even had a long drink, take it outside. In many cases, there will be results within a few minutes. Don't drag this out, however, if you've been outside for 10 minutes and nothing has happened, say nothing and bring the puppy back inside the home.

2. To begin with, puppies will simply urinate and defecate where they are. There is usually no warning when the bladder needs relief, and you should just resign yourself to cleaning up urine for a time. However, when a bowel movement is imminent, you may see your pup circling around and acting a bit agitated. Before the puppy actually starts to defecate, pick it up and take it outside. Lifting the puppy will cause a temporary interruption in the process, generally enough to allow you to get to the yard. Pet and praise the Catahoula pup as soon as a deposit has been made in the yard.

3. If you see the puppy urinating, you can also pick it up and take it outside as quickly as possible. You may have to clean up a trail, but if the puppy does manage to finish urinating outside, be lavish with praise.

'Grab and Run' can be quite effective as a housetraining method as long as you are actually able to manage it. This will work best with those who work at home or those who are retired. Women who are homemakers can also take advantage of this technique to housetrain a new puppy. As with paper training, punishment or scolding has absolutely no place here, and will only be counterproductive.

Housetraining by Crate

Crate use for dogs and puppies has become something of a fad over the past few years, and some dog owners seem to view the crate as an essential piece of equipment. Crates can be useful for housetraining a Catahoula, especially if the owner is unable to watch the puppy constantly. However, if you must be out of the house for an extended period, do not use the crate for housetraining. For those who do decide to use a crate to help housetrain their puppy, there are some factors that should always be kept in mind:

1. The size of the crate must fit the size of the puppy. A crate that is too small will be uncomfortable to the puppy, and could actually cause it to eliminate from stress. This will create a mess that you will have to clean up. A crate that is too large will also be a problem because there will be enough room for the puppy to use part of the crate as a bathroom without getting dirty itself.

2. When using a crate for housetraining, it's advisable to also feed the Catahoula puppy in the crate. This should be done according to schedule, as you would if you were

using any other housetraining method. Once the puppy has eaten, take it out of the crate and to the area where you wish it to eliminate. You will usually see results in a short period of time.

3. After the puppy has been brought back inside, put it into the crate again for about 20 minutes then take the pup outside again – your puppy will probably need another bathroom break then. Of course, if the weather is fine and you are able, you can stay outside with the puppy after it has first eliminated for some play, and to await the next call of nature.

The theory behind using a crate to housetrain a Catahoula is that a crate of the proper size will discourage a puppy from soiling it, and the pup will learn to control itself, at least a little bit, in time for you to take it outside. This method, like the previous, requires you to be on hand during the day to constantly monitor the pup and see that a schedule is adhered to. You should never expect that you can pack the puppy into a crate, leave for the day and come back to let the pup out after you've finished with your peregrinations – you will only come back to a crate filled with feces and urine, and probably a very dirty, smelly, and unhappy Catahoula puppy.

Chapter Three: Housetraining Catahoula Puppies and Adults

Handling Accidents

You should always be realistic about the probability of accidents. We have been lucky, but most owners will have to deal with house soiling even after it was considered that housetraining had been completed. Once again, do not react in any way other than to clean up after the animal; forget the rolled up newspaper or other forms of punishment, the puppy will have no idea why you are hurting them. It's also quite possible that you left the puppy alone for too long a time or it just became anxious – separation anxiety is a big cause of accidents.

The urine or feces should be removed immediately, and the area completely cleaned. You may want to use ordinary soap or detergent and hot water to clean up, and this is a good way to begin, but the organic compounds in the waste will continue to provide odor signals to the puppy unless you use an enzyme cleaner. Enzymes will break down and eliminate the telltale smells and make it much less likely that the pup will be attracted to the spot in the future. You may have to repeat the enzyme treatment several times. Never use ammonia to clean up the spot; it will only exacerbate the problem.

Male Catahoulas will sometimes begin to engage in marking behavior when they are about 5 months old. This is an instinctive reaction to staking out a territory. If you have decided to neuter the puppy, this should take care of the problem, but if you are leaving your male Catahoula intact and the problem persists, consider using a belly-band to control him. The belly-band will prevent him from performing the 'ceremony' that accompanies marking behavior, and positive reinforcement for urinating outside will probably eliminate the problem entirely in short order.

Look upon an accident as a 'one-off' occurrence, and simply keep up with whatever housetraining procedure you have been using. In all likelihood, the puppy will revert to using the outdoors or papers again without any problem.

Accidents are quite likely when you first bring your new Catahoula puppy or dog into the home. Expect that the pup will urinate. This is caused by excitement and/or the desire to claim the new location, and usually will not be repeated. Say nothing and clean up the mess, preferably with an enzyme based solution.

Housetraining accidents can also occur when a puppy or dog has been very ill. We have seen this in our Catahoulas when they required hospitalization for a severe illness. For some time afterwards, they were unable to control their bladders, especially when they were receiving subcutaneous fluids. Once they recovered, the problem vanished. I have never viewed these episodes as housetraining accidents, since the dog has been completely unable to control its bladder. This can definitely make it difficult if your dog is used to sleeping with you; we got around the problem by putting a piece of plastic under the area where our Catahoula was going to sleep and covering it with a large rag that could either be washed or tossed.

Housetraining an Adult Catahoula

Housetraining for an adult Catahoula that you bring into the home is basically the same as you would use for a puppy, although you will probably not use paper training. Keep in mind that some adult dogs, especially those from shelters, could well have some mental or physical conditions that might make training more difficult. You may be pleased to find out that your new family member is already housetrained and nothing more is necessary than to introduce it to the yard. However, there can also be times when you will need to actively housetrain your adult dog, and the steps to do so are not difficult to follow:

1. Begin by establishing an eating and elimination schedule right away; taking the dog outside every 2 hours is appropriate. This will help to regularize the dog's system and make it less likely that there will be accidents. It will also help if you give your adult dog 2 smaller meals a day, rather than only 1 large one. This keeps the digestive system more likely to be reliable.

2. As with a puppy, there may be an initial urination to mark territory, but this usually will not occur again and should be cleaned up without comment or fuss on your part. The adult Catahoula is in a completely unfamiliar situation that it doesn't understand and will take some time to adjust.

3. The more you are able to be around your adult Catahoula, the more likely that it will quickly comply with your housetraining wishes. Once again, rely on positive reinforcement for a job well done, rather than punishment.

4. If you change your Catahoula's diet abruptly, it could cause it to develop diarrhea. This could cause unintentional accidents. When changing your Catahoula's food, do so gradually to allow its body to adjust.

Chapter Four: Crate Training

Since dog crates are now looked upon as being an absolute necessity if you have a puppy or dog, it's amazing that dog owners were able to do without them for thousands of years and still have happy, well-trained dogs. Be that as it may, crate training is now looked upon as being essential to keeping a dog; as important as food, water, attention, and veterinary care.

It is quite true that many dogs prefer to find a small, secure spot in which to sleep or relax, and a crate can provide this – as long as the door is kept open. Once the door of the crate is closed, it becomes a species of cage or prison. Crate training can help in housetraining, confining the dog while in transit or during an emergency, or when trying to correct destructive behavior. However, those who view the crate as a place in which to leave a puppy or dog for hours on end should consider whether they are really prepared to own a dog.

Catahoulas are social animals, and require companionship and interaction with humans. One may ask, what is the point of acquiring a Catahoula, or any breed of dog, if the animal is going to spend long hours confined in a crate? One of the major reasons for getting a dog is to have a companion.

If you purchase a Catahoula puppy or dog from a breeder outside your immediate area, it will likely be shipped to you in a crate. You can use this crate to begin training, as it is probably an appropriate size for the animal. Acquisition of a pet from a local breeder or from rescue or a shelter will probably require that you purchase a crate yourself. There are several varieties of crate: wire, cloth sided, and plastic. The plastic crates generally consist of upper and lower sections that are held together with screws, and this type of crate may prove the easiest to use when you are beginning crate training.

There is no way to 'cheap out' when buying a crate for a puppy. You should purchase one that fits the pup's size and continue buying new crates that fit the puppy until it is an adult. Your Catahoula should be able to turn around in the crate and have enough space to stand and to lie down comfortably. There are problems with crates that are either too big or too small:

1. A crate that is too small denies your Catahoula the ability to stand up, turn around, or even settle down normally. The only thing the dog will want to do is to get out of it as quickly as possible. This situation often arises when owners don't want to spend money on progressively larger crates as their puppy grows. If purchasing successive crates is beyond your financial resources, then simply don't bother with a crate at all.

2. Crates much larger than needed present their own problems. Many owners think that they can 'get away' with buying a crate that will fit the adult dog, leaving the puppy in a room, in effect. With so much space, the puppy will usually choose to use part of the crate as a bathroom, especially if it's left in the crate for an extended period of time – it can just retreat to the farther end away from the mess.

One important thing to remember is that you should *never* use the crate as punishment. Your Catahoula puppy or dog will do all in its power to avoid using it, and will probably be noisy until you let it out. Animals that are crated as punishment will often eliminate due to stress, which will only mean that you will have a very unpleasant cleaning up to handle, possibly including the dog.

Beginning Catahoula Crate Training

Unless your Catahoula arrived in a crate, and often even if it did, you will have to get the animal accustomed to it. You can probably count on the natural curiosity of dogs to begin investigating the crate right away. If you have a plastic crate, it's a good idea to remove the top half to make the crate seem less threatening and enclosing. Once your Catahoula seems comfortable with the open-topped crate, you can put the top half back on again, but still keep the door open. Let the puppy or dog explore the crate for several days, and become used to it before you start any actual crate training. Puppies are a good deal more likely to 'take' to their crate before than will an adult dog that has never before been confined.

It's important where you place the crate in your home. If you place it several rooms away from where the family gathers, it will not only be inconvenient, but the dog will feel isolated and lonely. The crate should be where the dog can see people, at the minimum. You can put it under a table or between several pieces of furniture so that it won't be so obtrusive.

You must make the crate appear both unthreatening and appealing to your Catahoula:

1. If you can remove the top half of the crate, do so, and start putting treats in the crate to entice the dog to enter on its own.

2. Either remove the door temporarily or tie it open so that it doesn't accidentally close and startle your Catahoula.

3. Provide comfortable bedding in the crate so that your Catahoula will enjoy lying down inside it. Remember to change the bedding every week – dogs actually like something clean to lie down on.

4. Praise your Catahoula whenever it goes into the crate on its own.

5. Feed your Catahoula puppy or dog in the crate.

6. If the animal is too frightened of the crate to actually eat inside it, place the food dish outside near the crate. As the dog becomes used to the crate, you can move the food dish inside. The water dish should also be placed inside; one that attaches to the door of the crate will help prevent spillage.

Take all these steps slowly and never display any impatience or anger if things are not going as you believe they should.

Once the dog seems to be comfortable in the crate, and going into it freely, you can begin closing the door. At this point, don't latch it, so that if your Catahoula panics, it can just push out again. Only leave the door closed for a minute or two and gradually work up to longer periods, eventually latching the door. Always remember to put treats and toys into the crate and also to praise and treat after a successful period in the crate.

Crating for Housebreaking

Crates can be useful for housetraining your Catahoula. You can begin using the crate for this once your pet has become used to the crate and is eating in it regularly. Place both food and water dishes in the crate. Water should be available to your Catahoula at all times, but you should feed your pup on a schedule as soon as you welcome it into the house. Very young puppies will do best with 4 meals per day, and it's advisable to feed adult Catahoulas smaller meals twice a day rather than one enormous meal. This helps to keep the energy levels of your Catahoula high and will prevent it from becoming too hungry between feedings.

1. Put the food dish in the crate and close the door. A puppy will usually have to have a bowel movement soon after eating.

2. As soon as your puppy has finished eating, take it outside to eliminate.

3. It can take up to 10 minutes for results, so be patient.

4. If your Catahoula puppy does nothing within this time period, take it back inside, put it back into the crate, and take it outside again in about 20 minutes.

5. Praise the puppy for a job well done when results are produced.

6. The same process should be applied to the pup's water dish – as soon as the puppy has had a drink, take it outside.

The theory behind using a crate for housebreaking is that canines instinctively avoid soiling where they sleep. However, if you leave your Catahoula puppy in the crate for too long periods, especially after eating or drinking, there will be accidents. The same measures for housetraining will apply to an adult as they will to a puppy. Puppies that have grown up in a kennel situation are used to eliminating where they eat and sleep and will often use the crate to urinate and defecate, especially to begin with. Never punish your puppy for this, and try a different housetraining method for these pups, or keep an extremely close eye on what your Catahoula puppy is doing.

Curbing Destructive Behavior

Catahoula puppies and dogs can engage in activities that can cause damage and even destruction to the home and its furnishings. Puppies are probably the worst perpetrators of this because they are teething. To relieve the feelings of their irritated gums and assist the new teeth in breaking through, puppies will literally chew anything they can get their teeth on. In most cases, as we found ourselves, this destructive behavior will cease once the permanent teeth emerge. You can help to stop this inappropriate chewing if you provide acceptable chewing material for the puppy. We found that choo-hooves worked best for our pups – they enjoyed not only the hard texture that helped with their teething, but also the taste of the hoof.

Choo-hooves also stood up well to the strong jaws of our Catahoula puppies. Keep in mind, however, that even if you provide a mountain of chewing toys, your Catahoula may still gnaw on your furniture or footwear. It is always best to remove things you do not want chewed from the reach of your puppy. Bad tasting sprays or liquids are available to put onto furniture, but one of our dogs actually developed a taste for bitter apple.

Some Catahoulas will also continue inappropriate chewing behavior into adulthood. Destructive chewing in this case often arises from separation anxiety when the owner leaves the home. This occurs because of the strong feelings that the dog has for its owner; wild canids tend to 'pal around' with one another constantly, so being alone is a hardship for most dogs. The Catahoula will often relieve its anxiety by chewing up furniture, rugs, curtains, or anything else within reach. You will be surprised at how much trouble these canines can deliver.

Crating for destructive behavior, to keep your Catahoula confined when you, the owner, are not in the home, should only be used as a last resort. Never use the crate as punishment when damage has been discovered – you have to find a solution to the problem rather than discipline the dog.

Other ways of handling separation anxiety will be addressed later in this book. If the owner absolutely must use the crate to keep the dog from tearing up the house, the Catahoula must first be completely familiarized with the crate to begin with – no owner should think that they can simply stuff their pet into the crate before leaving for the day with happy results; you could easily find a damaged crate and an injured dog upon your return.

If your Catahoula has accepted the crate and you are going to use this to confine the dog while you are at work, it might be a good idea to hire a pet sitter to come during the day to let the dog out to use the yard and stretch its legs. Any dog that is going to be left alone for more than 4 hours should be visited by a pet sitter or neighbor midway through the day; could you avoid using the toilet for 8 or 10 hours? Confining a dog for too long a period is not only cruel; it can easily result in a crate full of urine and stools.

Catahoulas are not the best candidates for long term crate confinement, and leaving your dog in a crate, day after day, could easily lead to behavior problems. Another alternative can be to have a friend or relative take care of your Catahoula while you're at work; this will guarantee that your dog gets the human companionship it needs and leads a more normal life.

Like most dogs, Catahoulas will often become destructive when they are deprived of mental and/or physical stimulation. Catahoulas need exercise and stimulation every day, and providing these can help to prevent destructive behavior from arising in the first place.

Taking your Catahoula on a walk, as long as the weather is not excessively hot, can help to satisfy its exercise needs. It doesn't have to be a long walk either, around the block or down the street and back home will be fine. Playing with your Catahoula can also keep it mentally and physically sound, as can teaching your Catahoula tricks, something that will be addressed later in this book.

Owners sometimes, in the hope of prolonging the life of their pet, will put their Catahoula on a very restrictive diet. Some Catahoulas will actually become destructive because they are looking for something to eat. They will break into dog food bags or attack the garbage if they have not gotten enough to eat. If the Catahoula's ribs are showing or you can feel them too easily, it's likely that it is acting up simply because it is hungry. Try increasing the amount of food you are feeding your Catahoula, and the desperate chewing may stop. Space the meals out over the day so that it will be less likely to get peckish. Yes, Catahoulas do have a propensity to overeat and can become obese, but half starving them is not the answer, either. If you are undecided on what and how much to feed your Catahoula every day, speak with your veterinarian.

When a Crate Should Never Be Used

Many people find crates useful with regards to their Catahoula, but there are situations when your Catahoula should never be placed into the crate:

1. Sick animals should never be confined. The only exception to this is if your Catahoula is being treated for heartworm, and its activity must be severely curtailed to prevent further damage to your Catahoula's heart or lungs. Putting a sick animal in a crate is simply cruel and could seriously interfere with an animal that is in pain from finding a comfortable position.

2. A Catahoula with diarrhea is a disaster in the making if placed in a crate; likewise a Catahoula with a urinary infection. Catahoulas suffering from these conditions will be unable to control their elimination and will only soil the crate and themselves. The body has absolutely no ability to hold in liquid feces.

3. Hot weather is another time when your Catahoula should not be crated. Confinement in a crate during extreme heat can lead to dehydration and heat stroke. Your Catahoula could die quickly under these conditions.

4. A Catahoula that has damaged the crate in its attempts to escape should not be confined; eventually the dog will also injure itself. If you find part of the crate has been chewed, it is signaling a desperate Catahoula. When one of our girls was shipped to us, we found that her little paws were all scored and cut where she had tried to dig out of the shipping crate, which was relegated to the barn immediately. These were relatively minor injuries – dogs

can break teeth or even their jaws or tear out their claws attempting to escape from a crate.

5. Catahoulas with separation anxiety will not do well if confined to a crate; it will only magnify these feelings and make the problem worse. Putting a Catahoula with separation anxiety into a little box is basically inhuman.

6. If you live in an apartment house or in a neighborhood where the homes are close together, your neighbors will certainly let you know if your dog has been barking or howling for hours on end. In this case, do not crate your Catahoula again. Catahoulas will bark nonstop for hours if they dislike being in a crate.

When to Give Up

Some Catahoulas will accustom themselves to a crate without any fuss, and although I am not one who believes in the use of a crate except when the door is kept open at all times (or for emergencies or when traveling), this will be an issue between the owner and the dog. Remember, you do not have to use a crate – it could well be that manufacturers and retailers of crates have pushed this 'crate agenda' on dog owners, but there is absolutely nothing that dictates that you must use a crate at all. In my opinion it is nothing more than a fad, and hopefully will disappear as soon as possible.

However, some Catahoula puppies and dogs will never become used to being confined in a crate – these dogs will constantly whine, bark, howl, drool, claw, or chew at the crate to get out. And, the solution is to let them out. There is no law or universal rule that states that crate training is somehow necessary to the health or wellbeing of a dog.

A client of mine had a toy dog that was well behaved and completely housetrained, yet she thought that she 'had' to keep her dog in the crate during the day because it seemed to be the accepted practice. The dog whined constantly for months on end, and was completely unable to accept being kept in the crate, even though it was placed next to her chair. One has to ask oneself, why bother? What was the point in keeping a well-behaved dog in the crate at all?

What is the point of having a dog if you are going to confine it to a crate, especially if you put your Catahoula in a crate while you are in the home? As far as sleeping arrangements go, many 'authorities' state that dogs should be confined in their crate at night. This is wrong – your Catahoula should either sleep in your bed with you or sleep in a bed next to yours.

Catahoulas are not automatons or robots, they are intelligent, emotional living creatures that have evolved with humans and should be treated with the respect they deserve. We have found, with our Catahoulas that sleeping in bed with us has completely negated the theory that dogs will bite when awakened suddenly. They may do so because they are sleeping alone and so are insecure and will react fearfully when touched 'out of the blue', but if you think about it, dogs and wild canines nearly always sleep together. If the normal reaction to be jostled when asleep was to attack, there would be little sleeping done as there would be constant fights. Dogs get used to being touched when asleep under more natural conditions and don't react at all, shuffle a bit to one side to make room, or perhaps open a bleary eye. My dogs have even shared my pillow without any problem.

Chapter Five: Obedience Training

After housebreaking, obedience is the training considered to be the most important by dog owners. One thing that every owner should keep in mind is that a great deal of their Catahoula's 'bad behavior' actually stems from them, not from the Catahoula itself. Obedience training is actually not only about training the dog; it's about training you, the owner, to also act in a certain way. We humans tend to look upon anything the dog does wrong as being the dog's fault. To a certain extent, it undoubtedly is, but in many cases, the human partner has acted in the role of enabler, whether consciously or not. Raising a Catahoula in a responsible manner is just as important as raising a child well.

Patience, time, consistency, goals, and more patience are required for successfully obedience training a Catahoula. Always remember that the level of trainability will vary from individual dog to individual dog. All breeds have their characteristics that form the foundation of the mental and physical makeup of the dog, but breeding practices and environmental conditions, as well as what might just be termed the 'innate quirkiness' of some dogs can skew expectations. The receptiveness of the Catahoula to training is actually unrelated to the actual intelligence of a dog – some dogs have evolved to do multiple tasks or as hunting dogs and will be very receptive to training. Dogs which have historically been used for only one job can be more difficult to train. From my own experience, Catahoulas can present some obedience training challenges, in part because they do have a good measure of the stubbornness that is found in dogs of all sizes.

Obedience training can obviously be carried out by the owner, and this is what happens in most cases, and this can help to make the bond between you and your Catahoula all the stronger. However, there are professional trainers and behaviorists that can also be used to provide the training needed, especially when difficulties arise. Owners who avail themselves of professionals for training should realize that they will have to continue with some level of follow-up to maintain the training over time so that their Catahoula does not 'forget' what it has learned. If you never use the 'Come' command for over a year, it's not too likely that your Catahoula will respond when you finally do. You can make refresher lessons into a game too.

Why Obedience Train?

Owners may well ask, "Why bother to obedience train my Catahoula at all?" And this is a valid question, after all this does take time, dedication, and a high level of involvement. Even the amenable Catahoula can exhibit unwanted behavior that can make it less than an attractive and valued companion.

Obedience training is simply a good idea for several reasons:

1. A Catahoula that is well-trained will be able to go more places with its owner – it will understand how to behave when confronted by strange situations and people. A trained dog will be much less likely to be startled and remain calm wherever it is, and you will not have to worry so much about it behaving in an inappropriate or aggressive manner; and yes, Catahoulas have teeth and know how to use them if they feel it is necessary.

2. Obedience training can keep your Catahoula safer. All of us who own dogs know that there are times when the dog will act unpredictably – such as running out in the road unexpectedly. Even if you keep your Catahoula on a leash when out of the home, dogs can sometimes just dart out when a door is opened, or escape from a fenced yard. If your Catahoula has learned to 'stay' when directed, it's likely that it will at least hesitate before proceeding into traffic and give you the opportunity to reach it.

3. Well-trained Catahoulas tend to be more confident. They understand their relationship with their owner better, and are not as prone to fear or fear aggression in comparison to dogs that have been allowed to 'run wild'. Some Catahoulas are aware of their comparative size in relation to other dogs and people. This can affect their emotions and behavior around others. Obedience training can help to

overcome this tendency. Conversely, some Catahoulas will consider that they are the biggest dog going and will challenge larger or potentially dangerous dogs.

Starting Early

As with the young of any species, a Catahoula puppy will be much more malleable and trainable than will an adult Catahoula. From about the age of 8 to 12 weeks, your new puppy will be at the best age to form a strong bond with you, and will be especially receptive to your training program. As the old saying goes, "Strike while the iron is hot." Use this development window not only to bond with your Catahoula, but to begin training.

However, when starting obedience training at an early age with your puppy, you should be aware that the puppy is still a puppy, and will not only be full of energy and mischief, but also will have a relatively short attention span. You will require a few pieces of equipment for training: collar or harness, long leash, and treats. There are a few commands that you can start teaching your puppy as soon as it comes into your home:

1. Sit

2. Stay

3. Come

4. Down

These 4 commands will actually be sufficient for most Catahoulas to go through their life with; they will allow you to control your Catahoula in most situations. These commands are also the foundation of more advanced commands that might be needed or desired.

Because the puppy's attention span will be relatively short, keep the sessions short too – 10 or 15 minutes is long enough. You can conduct several obedience training sessions during the day rather than one long one, and always remember to be lavish with praise and treats when the pup does well. Completely ignore mistakes; calling your Catahoula puppy out for an error will only provide negative attention and make it more likely for that error to be repeated. Use obedience training as a way to establish trust in you and confidence in your puppy.

It's not only the puppy's attention span that should receive attention; your attention span and the limits of your patience are also important. Training a Catahoula puppy to do even simple commands like 'sit' can take dozens of repetitions, and if you get frustrated, your puppy will pick up on this and be even more difficult to train. As soon as you start feeling frustrated or angry, even if your puppy still seems ready to continue, stop the training immediately. Treat your puppy and spend some time playing with it so that it will look upon obedience training favorably. Like with any other dog breed, Catahoulas can sometimes not be the easiest dogs to train, but they can be trained successfully if you are willing to put the effort into it.

Not everyone will be starting with a puppy, however, many dogs are adopted when they are older, either from a breeder looking to get rid of extra animals, or from rescue groups and shelters. Because your adult Catahoula will inevitably be coming with some mental and/or physical 'baggage', you may have to spend more time training an adult than you would a puppy. When adopting an adult Catahoula, give it a bit of time to settle into the new surroundings before you begin active training. Once again, relying exclusively on positive reinforcement for obedience training will produce the best and most reliable results.

Basic Obedience Training for Your Catahoula

It's best, to begin with, to choose a spot to train your Catahoula where there will be few distractions; this will allow both of you to concentrate on the training. You don't necessarily have to use the exact same place every day, and it's probably a good idea to switch the locations, too, so that your Catahoula puppy or dog doesn't come to associate obedience with just one place, but as something that is to be followed everywhere.

Sit

The "Sit" command is probably a good place to start; it's something your pet does naturally and requires little effort on your part or your Catahoula's. Kneel or use a chair or stool to keep you at approximately the level of your Catahoula. Use a leash to keep your Catahoula from backing up during this lesson.

1. Hold a treat just above your Catahoula's nose so that it gets a good sniff, and then move it over its head towards the back of its body. Make sure you keep the leash short.

2. This motion will cause your Catahoula to lower its rump as long as it cannot back up since the leash is preventing backward movement.

3. Once your Catahoula's rump touches the floor, say "Sit" and give your Catahoula the treat immediately. The point here is to get your pup to associate the word with sitting and receiving a treat.

4. You can do this several times, but don't repeat until your Catahoula dog or puppy becomes bored and frustrated. When its eyes start to wander or it seems fidgety, break off the lesson.

5. Spread lessons over the course of the day to keep them interesting. If you're like most people, you probably found your school days boring to one extent or another, and this

interfered with your learning ability; the same will be true with your Catahoula, if it becomes bored, it simply will not absorb the lesson.

6. This will generally achieve good results within a short period of time, and your Catahoula will learn to "Sit" without any other control than your voice – you will not have to dangle treats over its head.

Stay

You don't need to wait until the pup or dog has mastered "Sit" before adding "Stay" to the lessons. This command may take more work than "Sit" due to your Catahoula puppy's desire to be with you, so have patience.

1. When your Catahoula is in the "Sit" position, start moving away from it slowly, while repeating the word "Stay". You can make motions with your hand to encourage your Catahoula to remain in that position.

2. If your Catahoula remains in position when you have gone even a slight distance from it, treat and praise. Try to reward your Catahoula before it actually starts to get up.

3. Gradually lengthen the distance from your sitting Catahoula, all the while giving the proper command.

4. When your Catahoula breaks the "Stay" command, simply return it to "Sit" and try again.

5. Break off the lesson at the first sign of frustration on the part of either participant. This lesson can be repeated several times during the day – short, more frequent lessons are much more effective than long, drawn-out ones.

Come

"Come" may be one of the easier commands for your Catahoula pup or dog to master; it wants to be with you, after all, so just build on this natural attraction for successful lessons. You will need a flat collar and long leash for this lesson.

1. Attach the collar and leash and put your Catahoula in the "Sit" position.

2. Give the "Stay" command.

3. Move several feet away from your pup and say "Come". Chances are that your Catahoula will move towards you, and be sure to treat and praise. Squatting down, rather than standing, will make your Catahoula even more eager to come to you.

4. If your Catahoula seems reluctant to approach you, give a small tug on the leash to get it moving, this is not any kind of correction, rather to just get your dog's attention. Do not drag your Catahoula towards you, this sends a negative message, such as anger. If your Catahoula comes upon receiving the cue, treat and praise.

The important things to remember when giving basic obedience training is to keep the training sessions short, especially for puppies, and always use positive reinforcement, in the form of treats and praise, to reward success. It will take numerous repetitions, in most cases, for your companion to understand what you want and to learn to respond to your commands. Never allow yourself to become angry with your Catahoula, it is counterproductive.

It's quite possible that you will run into some bumps and stops while training your Catahoula. Catahoulas can easily become tyrants in the home. Due to their bond with their Catahoula, owners can often allow them to get away with more bad behavior without realizing. Of course, it is extremely unlikely that anyone in the family home will be seriously harmed by your Catahoula, although they could injure a small child, but do you really want to live with a dog that growls and snaps, or even bites when it doesn't get its own way? Obedience training is one way to prevent this from happening without having to come down heavily on your Catahoula. Preventing problems in the first place is always much easier than trying to correct them.

Once a training session has been completed, spend some time playing with your pup so that it will come to look upon these sessions as a prelude to a good time. Remember that the best time for training to be conducted is while your Catahoula is young; not only because it will be most impressionable then, but also because negative behavior patterns have not been fixed.

Advanced Techniques

Once your Catahoula has been reliably trained for basic obedience, you might want to train it for more difficult training objectives. These are also valuable tools for helping your Catahoula behave well in a variety of situations, and once the basic techniques have been mastered, you will probably find it easier for both of you to proceed to the next training steps – both of you will have become trained.

Down

Placing a Catahoula in the "Down" position can be looked upon as the first of the more advanced obedience techniques. This will help your Catahoula behave better both in the home and outside of it. It can help to calm an overexcited Catahoula, or keep one that is injured or ill quieter. However, keep in mind that your Catahoula will look upon this as being a submissive position for it to be in, and may resist it more than it would the basic obedience commands.

Previously, it had been taught that the way to teach down was to force your Catahoula down by using the pressure of your foot on its leash, but this method should be avoided – it will only intensify your Catahoula's feeling of helplessness, or could spark aggression. This technique can be used when your Catahoula is either sitting (the easiest since the dog is halfway there) or standing.

1. Get your Catahoula into the "Sit" position. Place a treat in front of its nose and lower the treat to the floor. The Catahoula will naturally lower itself. As your Catahoula's body touches the floor, say "Down".

2. You will, of course, have to repeat this exercise quite a few times, but as long as you keep treating your Catahoula and giving it praise, "Down" will become part of your Catahoula's repertoire.

3. After your Catahoula has taken the treat while lying down, use another treat to bring it back to the sitting position, and repeat the lesson.

4. It can be a bit harder to get your Catahoula to lie down if it's standing, but repeated practice, using treats and praise will train your Catahoula to obey your command.

5. As always, suspend practice when your Catahoula's attention begins to wander.

Heel

There has been quite a bit of discussion over the past few years about whether it really is necessary to teach your Catahoula to "Heel". Some trainers advocate letting your dog circulate around you, within a narrow radius, rather than stick to your left side. While there may be some validity to this new train of thought, it does relinquish control of the dog to a considerable degree, which could prove to be problematic in certain situations. By teaching your Catahoula to heel, you will be keeping the human member of the partnership in the leadership position and make the dog easier to control. Teaching a Catahoula (or any dog breed) to heel is difficult, but it can be done with time, patience, consistency, and treats. Unless you plan never to take your Catahoula anywhere at all, especially around other people and dogs, teaching it to heel is essential.

You won't need much equipment to teach your Catahoula to heel; harness or flat collar (depending on whether a collar can slip over the dog's head), leash, treats, and perhaps a piece of tape. You can actually teach your Catahoula to heel without using a leash, but most people find it more convenient to use one.

Choke collars, shock collars, or prong collars are not necessary to teach any dog to behave properly on leash, they only cause unnecessary distress to the dog and are an unneeded form of negative reinforcement. Always remember that the leash is not to be used to yank on the dog, it's only there to keep it from straying during the lesson.

1. Stand with your Catahoula on your left side. Hold the end of the leash in your right hand. The slack will be taken up by your left hand. This provides you, in effect, with a very short leash, and this makes it much easier for you to control your Catahoula. You should also keep some treats in your left hand, out of sight, and they mustn't have a smell that your Catahoula is able to easily detect.

2. Say your Catahoula's name to get its attention. Your Catahoula should make eye contact with you. If it doesn't look up at you, you can touch the top of its head to draw its notice.

3. Tell your Catahoula to "Sit", then say "Heel" and take two steps forward. If nothing else, your Catahoula will probably follow the scent of the treats. If your Catahoula follows you, treat and praise it.

4. If your Catahoula doesn't follow you, step back and repeat the heel command, perhaps holding the treat closer to your Catahoula's nose. Remember that this is something completely new to your dog and it will take a while for this lesson to be learned.

5. Repeat the two steps forward until your Catahoula can do this reliably, then increase the distance by two steps. Every time your Catahoula is able to follow the "Heel" command, increase the distance.

6. Vary the lessons after your pet is able to heel on command over a distance of 20 feet or so, by making turns or going around corners. Remember to practice these new additions one at a time until your Catahoula is comfortable doing them. As training progresses and your Catahoula heels well, try introducing distractions such as the neighbor's children or another dog. If your Catahoula shows any inclination to break the command, repeat "Heel" and direct your Catahoula to "Sit" to get it back to its mental starting point. Once it sits down, say "Heel", and continue as before.

7. As your Catahoula becomes more proficient in heeling, you can start cutting back on the treats; eventually you will rely entirely on the command and a word of praise.

Ideally, training your Catahoula to heel will proceed without any problem, but only the most rosy-eyed optimist would think that, and most of you will experience a glitch or two along the way. Unless you have a particularly stubborn Catahoula, it will learn to heel in time. Intimidating your Catahoula will not work (and could serve to make it aggressive), stick with positive reinforcement and things will work out, although you should be prepared to work with your Catahoula for a long period of time when teaching this. There are some common problems that will often arise during training, however:

1. If your Catahoula just doesn't seem to be paying attention to your left side, stick a bit of tape onto your side, at the height of your Catahoula's head – this will often be enough to help it focus on where it should be.

2. Don't be surprised if your pup lunges forward as it usually does when on leash. Don't pull on the leash or yell, simply stand firm. Your Catahoula is on a very short lead (or it should be) and won't be able to go far. Turn your body in the opposite direction; your Catahoula will have to follow without the need of any obvious force on your part. Give your Catahoula the "Heel" command again, and if it remains at your side, take two steps forward and treat if your Catahoula follows.

3. You can also use the 'stand and turn' if your Catahoula has become distracted by something and tries to wander away.

4. Catahoulas that have become bored make very poor pupils and if you see your Catahoula yawning or becoming obstinate, suspend the lesson – continuing it when your Catahoula refuses will just reinforces your pet's stubborn behavior. Needless to say, don't give your Catahoula a treat now.

Once your Catahoula has mastered the "Heel" command you will be able to confidently take it with you wherever you go. Not all Catahoulas will learn at the same level of speed, and some may need much more intensive work than others. The key is to be liberal with praise and treats, and to break off a session when either of you is becoming frustrated. A younger dog will, of course, be quicker to catch on to what you want, but a dog of any age will be able to learn this command if you are willing to take the time and effort to teach it.

Obedience Classes

Puppy or dog obedience classes are another training option that has worked well for many people who own Catahoulas. These are classes that can be a good idea in a number of ways: you and your Catahoula will be doing the lessons together, and your pup or adult Catahoula will learn how to get on better with other dogs and with strange people. Be sure that your pet's vaccinations are up to date before enrolling in a class, and never take your dog there if it is showing any signs of illness.

Although most people who opt for classes do just fine with a group arrangement, there are times when the owner may want to schedule private training classes. A Catahoula that has serious behavioral problems should not be in a group class, nor should a Catahoula that is showing a high level of fear and anxiety. In these cases, an animal behaviorist can help you work with your pet to overcome their problems and become obedience trained. A fearful or aggressive Catahoula will be more likely to keep itself under control when it has become more confident through obedience training.

If You Decide to Use a Trainer

Sometimes, an owner either doesn't have the time, knowledge, or patience to provide adequate obedience training for their Catahoula. An unruly Catahoula, even a small one that is displaying problem behavior, will often wind up in a shelter unless some kind of training is provided to help the animal learn how to adjust itself to the household. While training your Catahoula yourself is obviously the best answer since it helps to establish a close relationship between you and your Catahoula, a trainer can be used if necessary, and is certainly an option if you are ready to give up on your Catahoula.

There are some very important things to understand when you are considering a trainer, and the first is that there are no laws or statutes that control dog training – literally anyone can call themselves a dog trainer regardless of how competent or skilled they actually are. You can run into a trainer that is absolutely the top in their field, or a total incompetent that will harm your dog. Before you consign your Catahoula puppy or dog over to a trainer, there are some things that should be checked beforehand:

1. Ask to inspect the trainer's facility. It should be clean, at the very least; a place that stinks of dog feces and urine, or

that has piles of garbage around is not a place you want to leave your Catahoula.

2. Ask the trainer if he or she has any kind of certification or has attended any seminars on dog training, these could lend some credence as to their ability to train your Catahoula.

3. Pin the trainer down on exactly what kind of training methods will be used – a red flag should go up if the person is vague about this; he or she probably doesn't know what they are doing and are just looking to make a quick buck.

4. Ask what kind of training equipment will be used, if any; mention of shock collars, prong collars, nose boppers, or choke collars should have you heading out the door as quickly as your feet can carry you.

5. Any trainer who mentions that your Catahoula might have to be euthanized should be avoided. This person obviously has no affinity for dogs and could well harm your Catahoula.

6. A trainer who claims that their results are guaranteed will literally be 'talking out of the other side of their hat'. Even the best trainer will not absolutely be able to produce completely positive results with every dog - there are simply too many factors involved for promises of this kind to be made.

7. Pay attention to your instincts about the trainer. If the person makes you uncomfortable, look elsewhere for help. Someone who seems 'creepy', loud-mouthed, or aggressive is not someone with whom you want to leave your Catahoula. Any trainer who makes even the vaguest of sexual overtures to you should be avoided immediately.

8. If the potential trainer seems to be under the influence of alcohol or drugs, vacate the premises immediately.

Even if you find the perfect trainer who fulfills your every expectation, you will still have to use the commands your Catahoula has been taught on a regular basis – the dog will simply become accustomed to not hearing and obeying the commands if you don't use them. You certainly shouldn't expect your Catahoula to heel perfectly if it hasn't heard the command for 10 months; keeping your Catahoula current on the lessons learned will be up to you, unless you want to keep returning your Catahoula to the trainer for refresher courses.

Training Collars

There are a number of different kinds of collars or harnesses that are used for training dogs. You will be using either a harness or a collar when teaching your Catahoula obedience.

1. Flat collar. This is the old reliable leather or nylon collar that lies flat around the dog's neck; it is adjusted to the neck and will neither tighten nor loosen when on the puppy or dog. Attached to a leash, this collar provides a great deal of control over the animal. You should be able to get two fingers under the collar if it is adjusted correctly. A collar that is too tight can restrict the dog's breathing and be uncomfortable, while one that is too large could just slip right over the head.

2. Choke collar. A choke collar is a length of metal chain with rings attached at either end. By slipping part of the collar through one of the rings, the owner will have a loop that can be fitted over the dog's head. A leash is attached to the free ring. These collars, unlike flat collars, can be easily tightened when the owner wishes to correct the dog. Pulling on the leash will cause the collar to squeeze the dog's throat. These collars should release immediately to allow the dog to breathe. The correction can be slight, mainly to draw the dog's attention, or sharp, to cause pain and restrict breathing temporarily. Choke collars can damage your Catahoula's windpipe or spine, and they can also cause bruising.

3. Prong collars. Surely something out of torture chambers, prong collars are a species of modified choke collar with prongs on the inside. Like Martingale collars (used mostly for dogs with very narrow heads), prong collars are self-limited, and unlike choke collars, can only be tightened to a certain extent. There is obviously no way that this kind of collar will be used except to inflict pain on the animal during training. Pulling on the leash will tighten the prong collar, pressing the points into the dog's flesh. These collars can cause serious injury to a Catahoula – in the past, the tracheas of dogs have been pierced by these collars.

4. Shock collars. Many trainers rely on shock collars when working with Catahoulas simply because the trainer does not have to be next to the dog for the collar to work, they have a variable range, depending on the collar. There are different 'correction' levels with most shock collars, ranging from a mild vibration to one step below electric chair. Some breeds will be able to ignore any 'stimulation', rendering the collar completely useless. Shock collars have a small box with prongs that are fitted so that the prongs are just pressing against the center of the Catahoula's throat (contact with the dog's flesh is necessary if the shock is to be felt). These collars should only be left on for a short period of time. They can cause irritation and even burns to the skin if overused.

5. Front clip harnesses. Most harnesses have the attachment for the leash over the dog's shoulders. While the most common of harnesses, it also makes control of the animal more difficult. Front clip harnesses have the leash ring in the front, right under the dog's head. This does provide you with a better measure of control over your Catahoula, but admittedly is still not quite as effective as the flat collar. You will also have to keep the leash short as the dog can become entangled in it if it's too long.

6. Tightening harnesses. Like the ordinary front clip harness, these have the leash attachment in the front rather than on the dog's back. However, they do allow you to cause a slight measure of discomfort to your Catahoula if it is not obeying when you pull on the leash and tighten the harness. While this is obviously not as nasty an apparatus as prong or choke collars, remember that you are still dealing with your companion, and so tightening the harness is probably simply overkill for your Catahoula.

Don't Expect Miracles and You Won't Be Disappointed

While it is completely true that the great majority of Catahoulas can be trained to obedience to one degree or another, there are also times when the owner is disappointed in the results, or lack thereof.

Part of the problem could lie in unrealistic expectations. Before you get a Catahoula, analyze what you want out of a dog – do you want a dog that will just be content to buddy around within the house and yard, or do you want an active dog that will participate with you in outdoor activities, or are you looking for an active guardian of the home and property? These are important questions because no amount of training will be able to overcome the basic breed characteristics.

Chapter Six: Clicker Training

It may surprise you to learn that clicker training and the concept behind it had its beginnings about 60 years ago. Clicker training is based on conditioning principles that teach the dog to associate the desired behavior with a sound and a treat. The idea is that by using a distinguishing sound, different from human voices or the ordinary background noise, it would help to train any dog, including Catahoulas, more quickly and efficiently. Other noisemakers, such as whistles, were also contemplated, but the ease and simplicity of using a clicker has made this object the best choice.

When this form of conditioning was first proposed (actually by B.F. Skinner, and others investigating the conditioning process in both humans and animals), it was decided that praising the dog for doing something right with verbal praise or by petting, was too slow to provide an accurate reinforcement; the dog might have trouble understanding that the praise was relevant to the correct behavior. The distinctive 'click' is quick and easy to produce, and for this reason was considered to be superior.

It doesn't matter whether you are starting training with a new Catahoula puppy or teaching an old dog new tricks, clicker training could well be the easiest and least stressful way to train your dog for both of you. You will hardly need a pile of expensive equipment, either – all you need is a clicker, treats, and a leash. Some more sensitive Catahoulas, especially puppies, can be startled by the strong sound the clicker produces; most will get used to the sound quickly, but if you find that your Catahoula jumps every time you use the clicker, try substituting a retractable pen; the clicking sound that a pen produces is much softer than that of the clicker, but still distinctive.

Getting Started

The first step in clicker training is to get your Catahoula to associate the click with the reward – the treat. At this point, you will not be trying to train your Catahoula to sit, stay, or come, but merely to condition your Catahoula to realize that after a click is heard, a treat will be forthcoming. You can and should do this in different places of your home and yard, to accustom your Catahoula puppy or adult to recognizing the clicker wherever you are. You can even do this stage of the training while sitting watching your favorite television show in the evening.

Begin this initial stage with a good supply of treats (small pieces of something your Catahoula particularly likes will work best – remember, you aren't actually feeding your Catahoula now). If possible, start this when it's been a few hours since your Catahoula puppy or dog has been fed; it will be much keener to get the treats than it will be when its stomach is full. As with all dog training exercises, you will need to repeat this multiple times, but this learned association will lay the foundation for all of your future clicker training.

Don't overdo the repetitions, click and treat a maximum of 10 or 12 times, say, and then let your Catahoula relax and get up onto your lap; you can even do the click and treat while your Catahoula is snuggled up with you. Vary the time between the clicks, also, making some following on the heels of the previous click, but letting a minute or more go by before the next. Be sure to praise your Catahoula after the training session is over. Initial clicker training will be most effective and enjoyable for both of you if you have numerous short lessons throughout the day, rather than 1 or 2 long ones. The attention span of most Catahoula puppies and dogs is not overly long, and once the animal becomes bored the lesson will lose its meaning. Sessions of 10 minutes or so are best.

Using Clicker Training

How effective you are with clicker training at this point will depend on your ability to react quickly to what your Catahoula is doing. The same basic techniques that you would ordinarily use for basic obedience training can easily be incorporated with clicker use. For example, when you have successfully gotten your Catahoula into the "Sit" position, click and give the Catahoula a treat.

Make sure you act quickly; the lesson will be pointless if you are trying to teach "Sit" but you don't click until your Catahoula is in the process of standing up again; there will be no way that your Catahoula will be able to associate the click with sitting in this case.

There are considered to be 3 excellent ways to obedience train your Catahoula using a clicker and they are termed: catching, luring, and shaping. Active obedience training generally makes use strongly of shaping and luring, while clicker training makes it easy to add catching to the mix.

1. Catching might well be referred to as "Caught in the act." In this case, it will mean catching your Catahoula already doing what you want it to do. If you are trying to teach sit, give the command, then click and treat immediately when you see your Catahoula puppy or dog already sitting. Catching can be used for nearly any behavior you are trying to teach, such as "Come" or "Down". Rely on your Catahoula's normal activities to teach the behavior you want.

2. Teaching your Catahoula to lie down using basic obedience training often involves using a treat to get your Catahoula to lower itself to the floor. Dogs tend to resist going down because it puts them in a vulnerable position and they instinctively avoid this. Clicker training can make this somewhat difficult technique easier for your Catahoula to learn. This method is called luring because you are using

a lure, the treat, to get your dog to do what you wish. You will be following the same basic clicker idea here as you used with catching, saying "Down", and using a treat to get the animal to lie down, this time, however, you will be adding the click as soon as your Catahoula is on the floor, to be followed by the treat.

3. Shaping is used when more complex behaviors might be wanted. Rather than using the click and treat to reward an obvious behavior such as sitting, in this instance you will use your clicker to teach your Catahoula a varying number of small steps to attain an ultimate goal. If you want your Catahoula to be able to sit up on its hind legs and then offer its paw to be shaken, you will have to teach it first to sit, then to sit up, and finally to stick out its paw. Each step of the process will have to be taught before the next step is undertaken, which can make this a somewhat lengthy process, depending on what exactly is involved. Luring has been used to teach complex activities to service dogs such as putting clothes into a washing machine, taking them out, putting them in the dryer, and then putting the dried clothes into the clothes basket.

Clicker Training to Correct Unwanted Catahoula Behavior

Inappropriate behavior by your Catahoula puppy or dog can be easier to correct when you use clicker training. Make certain that your Catahoula completely understands the connection between the click and the treat before you begin. The sharp sound of the clicker draws your Catahoula's attention and makes it easier for it to focus on the task at hand. You will not be using the clicker when your Catahoula is engaged in inappropriate behavior (you will, of course, have to intervene with as little fuss as possible if it is chewing on an electric cord or destroying your favorite pair of shoes). In these cases, remove the object from the Catahoula without saying anything, or simply saying "No!", and then try offering a chew toy instead. If your Catahoula begins chewing the toy, click and treat.

Although it will take some time, your Catahoula will eventually learn to direct itself to approved behavior in order to hear the click and receive a treat. By responding to the positive reinforcement of the clicker signals, your dog will gradually unlearn the bad behavior. This will take time and patience on your part, so be prepared to stay calm and persistent throughout the 'unlearning' process. Keep in mind that the longer you have allowed negative behavior to continue, the longer it will take to correct.

Teaching Catahoulas Tricks

Catahoulas are intelligent dogs and are able to learn a wide range of tricks. Teaching your Catahoula tricks is not only a way to provide for a more amusing companion, but also a way for you and your Catahoula to bond more closely together. As with almost anything you are trying to teach your Catahoula, it is always important to use patience and positive reinforcements to achieve the best results. Dogs in general try to please their owners, and this is even more evident in dogs that are used exclusively as companions.

You will probably find that the best results when teaching your Catahoula tricks will be to use a clicker. If you haven't used clicker training before, please read the section in this book that deals with this. Once you and your Catahoula have the basic clicker principals understood, you'll be ready to start teaching tricks to your Catahoula. While there are obviously dozens of tricks that you can teach to your Catahoula, it's probably best to start with a few simple ones, then move onto more complicated tricks. Your Catahoula should also be obedience trained before you even consider teaching tricks to it, so if you haven't done this yet, backtrack and take care of that first; many of the tricks will be built on basic obedience commands.

1. **"Shake"**. This is the old reliable trick and is one of the easiest to learn, as your Catahoula probably already has a tendency to give you the 'paw of friendship'. Get your Catahoula to sit, then hold a treat just out of reach. If your Catahoula gets up to get the treat, return it to the sit position. Most dogs will start to paw at the air in order to get the treat, and this is precisely when you should click if you are using a clicker, say "Shake" and give the dog the treat. As this is a natural action on your Catahoula's part to

begin with, "Shake" will undoubtedly be simple to teach, and it won't be long before your Catahoula is offering its paw on command.

2. **"Roll over"**. Your Catahoula must know the 'down' command in order to learn this trick. After putting your Catahoula into the down position, hold a treat in front of its nose then move it to one side or the other. If your Catahoula gets up, tell it 'down' again. In time you will be able to get your Catahoula to roll over onto its side. Treat and praise immediately once this step has been done. The more difficult step will be to get your Catahoula to roll over onto its back, but repetition will accomplish this in time.

3. **"Push"**. I've taught my dogs this so that they can get into the house easily during cold weather; sometimes I'll be waiting outside for one to finish its business while the other is already done. Leave the door nearly closed, and encourage your Catahoula to get as near to it as possible. Once your Catahoula's head touches the door, say "Push, push". Don't hesitate to help your Catahoula along by giving a gentle shove while giving the command. Some Catahoulas might be a bit hesitant to push against the door, but should come over fairly quickly.

4. **"Pull"**. You can also teach your Catahoula to open doors. The key to learning this trick is to attach a cloth to the handle of the door; this will give your Catahoula something it can get a hold of. This trick will be easier to teach if you

have already played tug of war with your Catahoula. If you have not done so, start out by doing this, and when your Catahoula tugs on the cloth or rope, say "Pull". It shouldn't be too difficult to get your Catahoula to tug on the rope or cloth that you attach to a door. You might want to be careful about putting a cloth on the refrigerator door, however.

5. **"Take"**. All dogs have a prey drive, and it's obvious that this instinct is still a part of their nature. Put a toy down on the floor near your Catahoula and as soon as it grabs the toy, click and say "Take". Provide a treat and praise, and soon your Catahoula will pick up a nearby object upon your command.

6. **"Bring"**. The flipside to the 'take' command is 'bring'. Once your Catahoula has picked up the toy or other object on your 'take' command, you will want to teach it to bring it to you. You probably won't get your Catahoula to bring the toy to you the first time, so use increments to achieve this trick. Tell your Catahoula to "Bring", and if it takes even one step towards you, click and treat. It won't take too long for your pup to associate moving towards you with the toy with the command and a treat. Be sure to be lavish with praise once your Catahoula delivers the toy to you.

7. **Bringing specific objects**. In addition to bringing a toy to you, your Catahoula can also be taught to bring specific objects. Yes, your Catahoula can be taught to bring you

your slippers or the newspaper or any other thing that this dog can reach and handle. Those who require a cane to walk can teach their Catahoula to bring that to them. The first step will be teaching the Catahoula to associate the object with the word, and once that has been accomplished, you will have to combine that with 'take' and 'bring'.

As with nearly all forms of dog training, your Catahoula will do best if you use positive reinforcement exclusively for teaching tricks. And remember, once you or your Catahoula start to get frustrated, irritable, or lose patience, stop training immediately and do something pleasant together.

Catahoulas as Therapy Dogs

People often confuse service dogs with therapy dogs, and while both branches of interaction provide benefits to us, there are some fundamental differences between the two:

1. Service dogs are dogs that are specifically trained to perform tasks that will help a disabled person function more normally. Those who are in wheelchairs, blind, or deaf are those who are most often seen with service dogs. The training of a service dog is a long process as the dog has to learn many different commands and understand how to do a number of different tasks. Training for a service dog begins in puppyhood where the dog first learns to respond to positive conditioning. Obedience training and

training for a specific role will follow when the dog has become older; all in all the process can take up to 2 years, depending on the type of service the dog will be providing. We have all seen service dogs guiding a blind person or pulling along someone in a wheelchair, and in general service dogs belong to the larger, stronger, more biddable breeds of dog.

Those who suffer from epilepsy can be warned prior to a seizure by their dog, and if they do have one away from home, their dog can protect them from muggers or other malefactors. Service dogs for deaf people do not necessarily have to be large dogs, a medium sized or small dog will do just as well.

Service dogs are usually easy to identify by the jackets or collars that they wear to demonstrate their status and they are allowed on public transportation and in any public building, even in hospitals, barring operating theaters. Renters cannot be barred from having a service dog in their apartment.

2. Being a therapy dog is a discipline where the Catahoula may be able to do well. Catahoulas have a natural affinity for interaction with people and this can certainly be used to good effect in work as a therapy dog. The training for a therapy dog can actually begin at any age, and nearly any breed of dog can be utilized. Smaller dogs can be ideal because of their portability and ability to be placed right

with the target individual. Larger dogs have also been known to do well in this arena.

The purpose of a therapy dog is basically to provide some unconditional affection and emotional support for people who may need these. Although any friendly animal such as a cat, rabbit, guinea pig, or miniature horse can be used as a therapy animal, dogs are the most frequently encountered in this role, due to their trainability and desire to interact with people. While obviously performing an excellent job, therapy dogs are not accorded the same unlimited access to public buildings and transportation as are service dogs.

Therapy dogs have proven themselves to be valuable over and over in a number of different situations. Catahoulas have been brought to hospitals and nursing homes to bring a bit of spark to an otherwise dreary situation. Many of the inmates in nursing homes will show an uptick in responsiveness after they have had a Catahoula sitting on their lap, just happy to see them and giving them some kindly attention. It's not an exaggeration to say that a visit by a therapy Catahoula is probably something that people in trying conditions, such as a nursing home, really come to look forward to.

If you are interested in having your Catahoula work in therapy, the first thing to do is to make certain that it is completely healthy; the dog should be current on all vaccinations. Rabies vaccinations are required for all therapy Catahoulas, and other vaccinations might be required by local ordinance; you will have to present proof that your Catahoula has received a rabies shot, at the very least, but your veterinarian should be happy to provide you with one. Obedience training is a must for any Catahoula (or any dog) that will be used as a therapy dog. Dogs that are used in therapy will be confronted with unusual and sometimes noisy conditions, as well as a number of strange people; a Catahoula that is well-trained will be much more likely to take these scenarios in its stride. Needless to say, early socialization is an absolute must for therapy Catahoulas.

There are several associations that will provide therapy dog training for your Catahoula, some of which will provide free training, and others that will require a fee. It is also possible to train your Catahoula for therapy work yourself, but it will have to be tested for competence and reliability. Your Catahoula must be able to tolerate loud, sudden noises without panicking, numerous people moving around in a strange setting should not bother your Catahoula, the sight of another dog (or any other animal) at the facility should be handled calmly, and unfamiliar equipment such as crutches, wheelchairs, gurneys, and IVs with monitors should not startle your Catahoula.

Your Catahoula should also be able to tolerate handling by people who may have limited mobility or difficulty controlling their movements; the very young and very old will fall into this category.

Once your Catahoula has passed the test, you and your dog are ready to begin providing help in a number of ways. Catahoulas can be led right onto a bed or to an individual without any problem.

1. People in hospitals can easily become depressed, but a visit by a therapy Catahoula can help to lift their spirits. Your Catahoula will also help to give them something to think about other than their current situation, and can reduce the stress they may be feeling.

2. Cortisol is a hormone released when someone is under stress and is related to a number of detrimental health conditions such as high blood pressure and heart disease. A visit by a therapy dog has been proven to help reduce the level of this stress hormone in the blood resulting in a lowering of blood pressure and a slowing of the heart rate.

3. Therapy Catahoulas often help to get those who are in nursing homes and hospitals up and moving more. The benefit from a visit by a Catahoula lasts longer than the actual visit itself.

4. Basic motor skills also improve when Catahoulas are available for therapy work. Balance improves quite a bit, meaning that the person will be less likely to fall, and manual dexterity takes a turn to the better as well.

5. Visits to those undergoing treatment is not the only way that therapy Catahoulas can make a big difference, it's been found that children who are struggling to learn to read do much better when they read to a dog. No Catahoula is going to raise a fuss if a child stumbles over a word or hesitates, and the confidence and reading skill of young students who have a Catahoula as their audience increases greatly. No Catahoula is going to be judgmental or impatient at the way a child is reading.

6. People who are victims of a disaster are often in a stunned mental state, even if they are physically unharmed. A therapy Catahoula can help to calm these people down and help them to start sorting out their lives again. Our long association with dogs means that just being able to come into physical contact with one provides relief from even the most stressful of situations.

7. AAA – Animal-Assisted-Activities – refers to times when your Catahoula will be interacting with people who are having extreme difficulties with their motor skills, such as might happen after a serious automobile accident or after surgery. In this kind of therapy, your Catahoula will be helping with improving a specific problem, such as helping a patient recover use of his or her hand after an accident or surgery. Undergoing physical therapy can be very stressful, and often painful, but a little help from a Catahoula can help the session go more smoothly.

8. Students in high school or in college are often under a terrific amount of stress, especially during exams and tests. Concern about their futures because of a bad test result can really stress these students out, and actually make them perform much worse on the exam than they would have otherwise. Your Catahoula can help these students to relax and is certainly a much healthier way to relieve stress than turning to drugs or alcohol.

9. Humans are not the only beneficiaries of the therapy your Catahoula provides. It's been found that like the people involved, Catahoulas benefit from a release of endorphins and other 'feel good' hormones, which help them to be healthier too.

It is perhaps not surprising that the first therapy animal was a little Yorkshire Terrier named Smoky. She helped not only the soldier who adopted her in New Guinea in 1944 when he was ill in the hospital, but she also used the tricks her owner had taught her to help men who were brought in wounded from the battlefield. The doctor in charge of the hospital, Dr. Mayo, was intelligent enough to realize how beneficial Smoky was and let her stay in the hospital.

Your Catahoula can now help to carry on the proud tradition that Smoky started by providing therapy to those who need help. If volunteering at a hospice, nursing home, or hospital is too stressful for you, consider those other venues available for therapy dogs.

Chapter Seven: Training the Difficult Catahoula

Living with a difficult Catahoula is akin to living with a problematic human family member – life can be extremely difficult and uncomfortable for all concerned. Difficulty with Catahoulas can take several forms: aggression to people or pets, problem barking, soiling the house, hyperactivity, and destruction of property. Some, if not most, of these problems can be overcome with persistence and training. It is best to never ignore your Catahoula as this can lead to it exhibiting aggressive or other undesirable behavior, and this can make living with them a hellish existence.

People who have Catahoulas that are exhibiting behavioral problems are often the cause of these problems. Very often people choose the wrong dog for their lifestyle, or fail to train it properly. Some breeds are simply harder to train than others, and this can include Catahoulas.

You should also recognize that some dogs can also come with inborn behavioral problems that no amount of training can fix (often the result of inbreeding by irresponsible breeders in most cases). When dealing with a difficult Catahoula, you have to realize that whatever problems exist (and there can be multiple difficulties) will take time, patience, and often money to correct if you want to have a pleasant household companion.

It is also true that some Catahoulas (like other breeds of dog) are mentally deficient in one way or another – like people, Catahoulas can be born with mental disorders that will be impossible to correct. Other dogs can just be, well, stupid. Depending on the nature of the mental state that is interfering with training, some Catahoulas, even those that are slower than the average, and seemingly impossible to train, can still make good and loving companions.

As with most training in regard to dogs, not only is the breed of dog that you choose important, but the age at which you get the dog is equally important. The best time to get a Catahoula puppy is between 7 and 12 weeks of age. At this point, the puppy has learned the basics of pecking order from its mother and siblings, and will be at the perfect age to adjust to living in a human household and bond with you. Puppies younger than this often exhibit training problems later, simply because they have missed out on this important 'natural training', and juvenile or adult Catahoulas that are brought into the home when they are over 3 or 4 months old (if they have just been confined to a kennel without much human contact) may always exhibit a wild dog mentality, and they will be unable to be trained at all.

A neighbor got a puppy when it was 8 months old. Prior to this, the dog had been kept in a small pen where it was able to watch its mother chase cars and trucks every day. Not only this, but the breeder spent literally no time with the dog at all, it had no contact with humans. This was the behavior that the dog learned, and although my neighbor tried literally for months to train the dog not to chase vehicles, it was impossible to break the habit. The last straw was when it actually attacked a car, biting at the tires and throwing itself at the car's windows to try to get to the people inside. After that, the dog was kept on an airline cable to give it plenty of room to run, but an inability to reach the road. This dog was never comfortable inside the home and always wanted to get outside, and exhibited on-again-off-again aggression towards the owners. Rather than offload the dog onto someone else, however, or have it put down, they did give it as much freedom as possible, as well as taking care of its physical needs. This dog never wanted to spend much time with people at all, and if free would range literally miles from the home, leaving its signature hole with a rock in it to mark the extent of its travels.

Catahoulas with a wild dog mentality find it very difficult to bond with people. This is not the dog's fault, it is the fault of the breeders, but the wild dog syndrome is nearly impossible to overcome – the die is cast. A Catahoula with wild dog syndrome can still be a fairly decent pet, however, the instincts of the breed are to be companionable with humans, so as long as you keep strict controls over your Catahoula, especially when it is outside the home, chances are that you and your Catahoula will be able to get through life together.

Is There a Solution?

If you have chosen a Catahoula, and for whatever reason, you are unable to train it, and it fails to live up to your expectations, you will eventually have to make some decisions, based on a number of factors.

1. The nature of the training problem will play a large part. A Catahoula that simply cannot or will not learn basic obedience commands, but that is otherwise a fairly well-behaved dog that gets along with the family will not present as thorny a problem as a dog that growls, snarls, or bites. Aggression towards people or other pets is dangerous and cannot be tolerated.

2. The size of the dog is also important – for example, a small dog in comparison to a larger dog would pose less of a threat. Either way, children will have to be kept away from a Catahoula with aggression problems, and should never be left alone with it under any circumstances.

3. Are you willing and able to devote more of your time to intensively trying to train your Catahoula? Most of us, unfortunately, have little free time available, so unless you

do have the time and patience to devote to training your Catahoula, you may simply have to give up on training. Training a difficult Catahoula can take weeks or months, although Catahoulas and other dogs with behavior problems can often become valued pets, the big question is whether you have the time and patience to do so.

4. Animal behaviorists can often help with any kind of training problem. This can range from housetraining to obedience to agility, and whether you come to rely upon one for helping with your Catahoula will depend not only on the problem behavior, but also on how dedicated you are to training the dog. If your Catahoula is consistently exhibiting aggression, however, you should consult an animal behaviorist. You can still be sued if your Catahoula bites a visitor and a passerby on the street. However, animal behaviorists do not offer their services free of charge, and using one of these specialists can cost quite a bit of money. The possibility that you might have to rely on an animal behaviorist to cure your Catahoula of serious behavioral problems, and the cost of this treatment, should also be taken into consideration. Will you be able to afford it?

Those who feel that the Catahoula's training problems, while perhaps insurmountable, are something that can be accepted and lived with, will likely keep their dog and come to terms with its behavior. The real sticking point will be where the dog's behavior is overly aggressive. If your Catahoula has bitten you or anyone else, a consultation with your veterinarian is essential, not only to rule out disease or injury, but also to advise you on the best course to take. A bite, even one that is not serious, should be seen by a doctor as soon as possible, to lessen the chances of infection.

Chapter Eight: Behavioral Training

All of us hope, when we get a Catahoula puppy or dog, that it will turn out to be the perfect pet of which we were dreaming. Unfortunately, just as the behavior of human beings often leaves a great deal to be desired, so can the behavior of the canines we bring into our homes. Adverse behavior can cause us to become angry, frustrated, and can lead to the pet being consigned to a rescue group or placed in a shelter, often to be euthanized. Before these steps are taken, however, behavior training might be the answer to the problem.

Behavioral training can be looked upon as the training that must be done when obedience training has either failed or has not been done in the first place, and can, in many cases be corrected.

In most cases, poor behavior on the part of the Catahoula can be traced to poor training, or no training, while the dog was young, and as long as the Catahoula is mentally sound, and you have the time and patience to curb the inappropriate behavior, you can often wind up with a well-behaved dog. However, in some cases, abuse while the dog was young, or poor breeding practices will make behavioral training difficult or impossible. Owners will sometimes come up against a Catahoula that is simply mentally defective in one way or another that will make instituting proper behavior impossible.

The fad for "line breeding" has often resulted in dogs that may meet a physical standard for conformation, but that have lost the mental traits often associated with the breed. For example, there are a range of breeds that became notable for their extreme good nature, but because some breeders bred siblings and cousins together, or even bred parents to their offspring, conditions such as 'sudden rage syndrome' now afflicts them.

Dogs that are subject to sudden rage syndrome (idiopathic rage, over-aggression) are not responsible for their actions and are unable to control them when the aggression is triggered – sometimes there is no trigger at all, there is just a suddenly launched attack on whoever is unlucky enough to be near the dog. The sad thing is that their genetic makeup is defective, and at this point in time cannot be corrected. Some vets will prescribe medication to try to control this behavior, but the results have been mixed. Some have likened sudden rage syndrome to epilepsy, especially as the dog has absolutely no control over it.

Fortunately, most adverse behaviors that Catahoulas exhibit will respond well to behavioral training, and can help reform a dog that has proven itself to be a pest into a valuable and cherished family member. When using behavioral training, once again the focus will be on positive reinforcement, although verbal remonstrance may be necessary in some cases; avoid screaming, if you have to correct the Catahoula verbally, say "No!" in a firm voice, rather than ranting at the dog. Once again, too, patience and understanding will be required; anger and frustration have no place in behavioral training.

Before trying to actively correct unwanted behavior in your Catahoula, use obedience training to teach the basics of 'sit', 'stay', 'come', and 'down'. Once your Catahoula has mastered these basic commands it will be ready to undertake the more difficult task of undoing problem behavior, and you will be much more likely to correct the behavior quickly and successfully. Regardless of what trainers who say that leadership training is wrong, simply by training your dog to obedience, you are being the leader; the dog is taking instructions from you, period. You can be a kind leader, there is nothing in the world to contradict that, and by being so you will not only help your dog overcome its problems, and give it more confidence, but will also establish that important bond between you.

Barking

Problem barking not only is irritating to you and the members of your household; it is also very irritating to your neighbors. Consider it the equivalent of having someone blaring music that you despised out of their house or apartment for hours at a time; having a problem barker can create social problems for you, and some people have even been sued because of the noise their dog was making. At the very best, if you allow your Catahoula to continue to bark and disturb the neighbors you are inconsiderate, and at the very worst, you could be subject to an enormous legal judgment against you, or by having an irate neighbor react harshly towards your dog. It has been known for dogs to have been poisoned or killed by neighbors at the end of their rope due to incessant barking.

Some owners seem to have a shut off valve in their ears that keeps them from being bothered by incessant barking, but others are just as annoyed as their neighbors might be. There are some measures you can take to help keep problem barking from starting in the first place, and to curb it if it does develop later.

Barking is a natural behavior to a Catahoula and is one of the ways that the animal communicates. However, be aware of this as you could find yourself with a Catahoula with a big mouth that barks excessively. Barking can be used to give a warning when a stranger approaches, a Catahoula might bark from joy when its master returns, dogs sometimes bark while playing, and some Catahoulas just seem to bark for the sake of hearing their own voice; these dogs will often bark when they are lonely or bored or afraid.

The first step to stopping problem barking is to determine exactly why your Catahoula is barking. If it is barking only when it's been left tied out in the yard by itself, the obvious solution is to bring the animal inside. However, most excessive barking will require a bit more work to overcome. As with most training, it will take effort and time on your part, but you will be rewarded with a quieter and more pleasant companion, and one that is less likely to get you dragged into court. Catahoulas with separation anxiety will also often bark excessively, and this problem will be handled later in this section. There are some steps you can take to curb problem barking:

1. Do not yell at the Catahoula to try to get it to stop barking, it will probably think you are joining in the fun.

2. If people walking by on the street are instigating barking while the dog is in the home, close the curtains. Barking at people when outside should also be discouraged – take the dog inside at once.

3. Reward quiet and ignore barking. This one can be difficult because it's hard for anyone to listen to a dog barking for hours without reacting. However, if you can bear it, wait until your Catahoula stops barking and then reward with a treat and praise. Needless to say, this approach might take some time, and will also require some forbearing neighbors, as well as nerves of steel on your part. However, do not expect neighbors to tolerate this

form of training indefinitely, at some point, they will complain again or call authorities.

4. If your Catahoula barks at other dogs, you can also help it to become 'numb' to other dogs by enlisting the help of a friend. This person should stand out of sight with his or her dog. You should have your Catahoula on leash. Make sure you have plenty of treats on hand and start giving them to your Catahoula even before your friend and the other dog makes an appearance. Once your friend shows up, stop giving treats when the Catahoula barks, but once it stops give the dog a treat. This technique will require quite a few repeats, as you can imagine.

5. When your Catahoula is barking, request that it be "Quiet" in a normal voice. Repeat the command until your Catahoula stops barking, even for a brief moment. As soon as the barking stops treat your Catahoula and say "Quiet". Eventually it will understand that a treat will be forthcoming if it stops barking.

6. Some Catahoulas will bark because they have failed to receive the stimulation and exercise that they require every day. Giving these dogs the exercise they need can often eliminate the barking problem.

7. Various types of collars are sometimes used to control barking. Collars that spray citronella have been effective for some problem barkers. Shock collars are controversial – a

woman I knew had to choose between getting rid of a problem barker and using a shock collar and did try the collar. She reported that the dog needed only one shock before it learned not to bark. However, few people have as good a result using shock collars and the dog often ends up with a damaged throat unless the collar is used properly and only for a short period of time. As noted previously, Catahoulas can easily ignore pain, so using a shock collar to control barking will probably be a waste of money.

Surgery to remove your Catahoula's voice box, debarking, is even more controversial than shock collars. This is probably better than having the Catahoula euthanized, but not much. Some dogs experience constant postoperative pain or have a greater chance of choking. And, like tonsils, some voice boxes will grow back, and the problem barking will start right up again.

Aggression and Biting

Aggression and biting are what are responsible (in addition to soiling the house) for causing the greatest number of dogs of any breed to be surrendered to shelters. These behaviors are completely unacceptable in a companion dog and must be curbed immediately. Although the theory of the human being the 'pack leader' has come under a cloud in some quarters of late, there is simply no denying that when the Catahoula looks up to the humans in the household, and considers that they are of a higher standing than it is, that there will be much less possibility of biting or aggression.

Being the 'alpha' in the home doesn't mean that the human is going to be punishing the dog constantly to keep it submissive. It means that the animal understands that the human is the ultimate arbiter. Any situation where the human is telling the dog what to do, or otherwise directing the dog's actions automatically places the human in the superior position; and this includes obedience training. As Dick Deadeye says in Gilbert and Sullivan's light opera Pinafore, "When people have to follow other people's orders, equality is out of the question." And this pertains to people and dogs too.

When we brought our first Catahoula home, she voluntarily exhibited submissive behavior to my eldest son. As soon as she saw my son, she instantly lowered herself to her stomach and crept up to him. When she reached him, she flipped over onto her side and exposed her belly. My son had done nothing to make her feel submissive – in fact all of us went out of our way to make her feel welcome and comfortable. This was instinctive behavior on her part. Catahoulas do not necessarily feel that we are 'dominating' them in any way by training them, or as can be seen with our first Catahoula, just by being there, they simply accept this as being normal.

In most cases, aggression and biting will never arise with your Catahoula puppy or dog, especially if you begin training a new puppy as soon as it comes into the home. Fortunately, most Catahoulas have an agreeable and balanced disposition, and the need for behavior control as regards to biting will never arise. However, it can happen and understanding how to deal with it is important for both you and your pet.

What might be considered 'normal aggression' in a Catahoula will usually begin with barking, which is a warning to you to back off now. If you ignore the warning, it will progress to growling, then snarling, where the teeth are exposed, and if you proceed with what you are doing, the Catahoula will probably bite. A bite in this case will usually be 'light' often not even breaking the skin, but it is still a bite. Even a very small dog can inflict a serious bite.

A Catahoula can deliver a very painful bite and this could very quickly lead to an infection. An adult Catahoula that suddenly starts biting must be taken to the veterinarian as soon as possible to rule out any physical illness or injury that might be causing this behavior. If your Catahoula checks out, and has no physical problems, then ask your vet to recommend an animal behaviorist – biting is too serious a matter for you to undertake correcting yourself; you could be injured if you attempt to correct your Catahoula.

If your Catahoula puppy begins to show aggression, it's possible to stop this before it becomes ingrained behavior, but it must be addressed immediately when the problem manifests itself. All puppies use mouthing as a form of play and communication. Under natural conditions, when puppies are engaged in play and one of them goes too far, the injured pup will squeal, and this causes the biter to back off. When this happens with you, you can substitute a rather loud "No!" or "Stop!" in the place of the squeal. The sooner you begin doing this, the less likely it is that your puppy will continue biting you. Do not strike the puppy, usually a sharp verbal reprimand will be sufficient. Most Catahoula puppies will really take such a reprimand to heart, and if you notice that your pup's feelings seem to have been hurt, do not try to comfort it, it understands that it has misbehaved and will come out of its funk on its own. If you comfort the puppy at this point, you will only be encouraging future bites.

In addition to verbally reprimanding your puppy, make sure that you have plenty of safe toys and chews on hand; if you notice the puppy starting to zero in on your fingers or hand, place a chew in the way. The idea of biting your hand will eventually fade from your puppy's mind as it comes to associate a toy or chew with using its teeth.

Catahoula puppies and dogs will exhibit possession over food and other resources (including toys, humans, and furniture), just as other dogs do. This is normal and natural to an extent as wild canids do have to protect their food from theft, but it has no place in the human home.

As soon as your puppy enters your home, begin training it to accept that you can take its food dish away if you wish, and can also take food, or other things, out of its mouth without any resistance. We have always done this with our dogs and have never had a problem with food aggression with any of them. They also take food from our hands in a gentle manner, rather than swallowing our hand up to the wrist.

1. Put your Catahoula puppy's dish in front of it and then take it away. If your puppy does not react in any way, reward it by returning the dish and praising your puppy. If your puppy growls, say "No!" in a loud voice and do not return the dish right away.

Repeat this over and over until even the most possessive puppy comes to accept that you have the right to its food whenever you want. This right should extend to every member of the human family, also; every human in the household has to be 'above' the dog in the family social order.

2. Your puppy must learn to accept that you can stick your hand in its mouth to remove food or any other object whenever you wish. Hand your puppy a treat and then

take it out of the pup's mouth. Most Catahoula puppies will simply accept this without demur, although some will need the same kind of training that is used with the food dish.

3. Never strike the puppy or intimidate it over this issue – if it won't cooperate on its own or with a simple "No!" command, physical force is not going to work, either, it will probably only exacerbate the problem and make the young dog afraid of you. Fear is at the root of many biting problems, so you do not want to make your pup afraid of you.

4. If your Catahoula puppy persists in biting you, consult your veterinarian immediately. A puppy should be responsive to your authority. Continued biting will only get worse as the puppy reaches adulthood, it will not get better.

Even the games that you play with your puppy can cause it to become more aggressive and more likely to bite you or others. Tug-of-war can also develop problematic behavior, so skip this activity with your Catahoula puppy. Once again, we never had any problems with this with our dogs. Providing sufficient exercise and play opportunities for your puppy can help to prevent biting from occurring in the first place.

Biting and nipping can also occur while the puppy is teething. Providing toys, nylon bones, and chew hooves when the pup is cutting teeth can help to direct them to acceptable chewing objects. If you are nipped, say "No!" and make a chewing toy available, praising when the puppy chews on that. Puppies will also be more likely to nip when they become overexcited while playing; keeping play times a bit shorter can help keep your puppy from reaching the nipping stage. Always remember to never leave a strong-jawed puppy alone with rawhide chews – the puppy might bite off a large piece and swallow it, resulting either in choking or intestinal blockage.

Aggression can also be manifested by your Catahoula puppy or dog denying you access to your couch, chair, or even bed. Don't let your puppy get away with this at all. It's fairly easy to remove a puppy from your furniture with a stern "No!" if you respond to the aggression instantly. Letting your puppy up on your furniture is up to you (we have always allowed it), but if you do allow it, make sure that your puppy realizes that it's a place to share. Don't hesitate, however, to reinforce good behavior with your puppy; give the pup treats and praise it when it behaves well, especially if it is already in possession and you move in with no problem. If you decide not to allow your Catahoula up on the furniture, make certain that it has comfortable pillows or beds available at various points in the home.

Biting in an adult dog is a serious and potentially dangerous problem. You, family members, other people, and other pets are all in danger from a biting dog. Thousands of serious bites are delivered every year by dogs, and fatalities also occur. A bite from even a small dog can be damaging and the wound could go septic. You should never consider that you are capable of correcting this problem safely by yourself, but must always seek professional assistance when attempting to deal with biting.

Car Chasing

To many dogs, a passing car or truck (or even a person or someone cycling) is prey to chase after, and this could include your Catahoula. All dogs have a prey drive to one degree or another, but it will be stronger in some breeds than in others. You might well have a dog that is totally blasé about cars or an easily excitable dog that cannot resist chasing them. Some dogs couldn't care a fig about traffic and will have no interest in chasing vehicles, while others will go after anything on wheels, including bicycles, scooters, and skate boards. Although a Catahoula should never be allowed to run freely outside in a densely populated area, there are times when this may happen. Remember as well that Catahoulas will have a natural instinct that is present within them that should be recognized.

Car chasing is extremely dangerous for your Catahoula; as it can easily be injured or killed by a vehicle. Even if your Catahoula is not killed, serious injury will mean that you will have to take it to the veterinarian for expensive care. Veterinary care can be nearly as expensive as human medical care, and a seriously injured Catahoula can easily rack up a number of costs in veterinary bills within a short period of time, especially if surgery is required to save your Catahoula's life. In addition to the direct cost to you and your Catahoula, you could also be liable for costs associated with an accident. Laws do vary from country to country, but in most cases, you can be sued if your dog causes a vehicular accident.

Many dogs are not simply content to chase after a vehicle, either, they will attack it. It's not uncommon for aggressive dogs to try to bite the tires or even jump onto the hood of a car – as can be seen from the behavior of my friend's puppy, described previously. This compounds the danger for the driver as well as for the dog.

Of course, the most logical and intelligent thing to do is to prevent car chasing from becoming a problem in the first place. Responsible owners do not open the door and let their Catahoulas out to 'do their thing' for the day, letting them back in at night to eat and sleep. Once you have decided that you are going to own a Catahoula, you are responsible for every minute of the animal's life – if you are unable to accept this responsibility, you should not own a dog of any kind.

Most states in America require that you have your dog leashed when it is outside with you. This will help to prevent car chasing from becoming a problem at all. If leashing is not required, then the owner should always be present with the dog when it's outside.

For those people whose Catahoulas have begun to show an interest in passing traffic, but have not yet begun to actively chase cars, there are several things that you can do to help prevent acceleration of the problem:

1. If car chasing has not actually begun, you can often redirect your Catahoula's attention. You will have to stand with your Catahoula, securely leashed, near the road. Whenever a car appears, distract your Catahoula with a treat, and praise it when it turns its attention to the treat.

2. Electric fencing cannot be relied upon to control your Catahoula's behavior; these dogs can often just ignore the discomfort and run right through the signal to chase the vehicle.

3. Reinforce obedience training in the home, the yard, and near the road. Make sure that you treat and praise every time your Catahoula obeys you and resists attempting to chase cars.

4. Keeping your Catahoula properly exercised (tired out) will also help keep it out of the road; a dog that has just returned from a long walk and intensive play session will be more likely to ignore traffic.

If your Catahoula is already chasing cars, there are a few things you can try, but ultimately you may have to seek the help of an animal behaviorist. Having someone throw water balloons at your Catahoula while driving past, turning your hose on your Catahoula, or using a noxious smelling spray only demonstrates that the problem is already beyond your control and you need professional help to deal with it. You should also examine how you are controlling your Catahoula in the first place – should this dog be outside without supervision.

The behavior of your Catahoula ultimately reflects on you, both morally and legally. No dog should be left to wander at will, and when outside should always be under the control of the owner, in a fenced yard, or on a chain (the least desirable situation, but still better than running free). Leaving your Catahoula outside on its own is hardly a wise thing to do under any circumstances.

Separation Anxiety

Our Catahoulas have always exhibited a high degree of separation anxiety, when away from us for even short periods of time. When our first Catahoula had to have dental work done she banged her head against the cage afterwards to such a degree that there were bumps and cuts on it. I even called the vet back the next day to ask about the damage and this was when they told me about her behavior. When she had to be hospitalized for a serious illness, the vet had to take her out of the cage and let her wander through the office so that she wouldn't harm herself. She also refused to eat at all, and only took a little water. We are fortunate in being at home constantly, and our constant presence has solved the problem for us, but others, who must be out of the home during the day, will need to find another solution.

Separation anxiety differs from simply inappropriate behavior because it only happens when you are out of the house. A badly trained Catahoula will soil the house right in front of you, while a Catahoula with separation anxiety will only do so when you are absent. Never punish your Catahoula for any messes it may have made in your absence; it will have no idea why you are scolding or hitting it -- the deed is long done. Finding a way for your Catahoula to deal with separation anxiety is the intelligent and humane answer.

There are several theories on why one dog will develop separation anxiety and another will be able to tolerate owner absences without a problem. The breed of the dog will have some bearing on this subject; many dog breeds, like the Catahoula, have developed to act as companions to humans, but any dog, of any breed can suffer from separation anxiety. Another factor in this condition appears to be that Catahoulas that have suffered an upset in their lives -- such as being returned to the kennel in which they were bred (often due to the breakup of their human family), or dogs that have been placed in shelters – will be more likely to exhibit anxiety when left alone. These Catahoulas undoubtedly fear that they will be dumped somewhere again, and because of their strong attachment to their new owners, are particularly liable to exhibit separation anxiety.

Dealing with separation anxiety to the extent that your Catahoula can comfortably and safely be left alone can be difficult, but it can be done in most cases.

1. Do not make a big production out of leaving the house; leave without even bidding the dog good-bye. Catahoulas with separation anxiety will quickly pick up on cues that you are getting ready to leave (picking up your purse, dressing in 'going out' clothing, shrugging on your coat). Minimize these cues as much as you are able, and also perform these activities at random times so that the dog does not automatically associate them with your leaving. For example, pick up your purse before dinner and then sit down to eat with it, or change your clothes before watching television.

2. Try to make a spot in the home where your Catahoula feels comfortable and safe while you're out. If your Catahoula likes being in its crate, you can use this, otherwise a specific room will do. If your Catahoula hates being in a crate, do not put your Catahoula into it while you are out, it will only make it more fearful and also likely to injure itself in its desperation to get out.

3. You can cut back on the amount of attention and affection that you give your Catahoula so that, frankly, it just doesn't like you as much as it did before and doesn't care if you go out. Personally, I feel that this is a completely wrong approach and defeats the purpose of having a companion dog in the first place. I consider this to be a solution that borders on the moronic.

4. Use short 'absences' to train your Catahoula to accept your absences. Leave the house for only a few seconds, and before your Catahoula can begin to misbehave, come back in again. Do not enter if you hear barking or howling or whining, wait until it's become quiet. Gradually lengthen the periods you are away until, hopefully, your Catahoula will accept your absence without problem. Don't make a fuss over your Catahoula when you enter, however, the point is to keep leaving and entering as uneventful as possible.

5. Some people will ask their veterinarians for tranquilizers for their dog. These should only be looked upon as a

stepping stone until you are able to change your Catahoula's behavior.

As with all aspects of dog training, trying to modify your Catahoula's separation anxiety just might not work out at all; there will always be a small percentage of dogs that are unable to mentally adjust to their owner's absence. There is no really easy solution here for those who have to be out of the home during the day, but Catahoulas that are unable to overcome separation anxiety can sometimes be left with relatives or friends or even placed in doggy daycare. For those who can do so, you might even take your Catahoula to work with you. This will only be possible with a calm Catahoula that will be little likely to disrupt the workplace, and is one more reason why it's a good idea to obedience train your Catahoula.

Digging

If you have ever gone out into your yard and twisted your ankle on a hole that your Catahoula has dug, or found yourself stammering apologies to the neighbor because your Catahoula has dug up a prized azalea plant, you understand how frustrating a dog's digging addiction can be. The digging instinct is present in all dogs, and that means that your Catahoula could also cause problems with digging.

As with most canine behavior, Catahoulas dig for a number of reasons; dogs left out in the yard for too long will dig from boredom or to escape; Catahoulas that feel too hot will dig to provide a nice, cool place to lie down; dogs dig to bury things; and a Catahoula might even be mimicking your gardening behavior. Catahoulas are known to be very good mimics of other creature's behavior, so finding a hole in your lawn could just be a case of your Catahoula doing some gardening on its own.

Obviously, the solution to problem digging in most of these cases is simply to keep your Catahoula inside unless you are outside with it. Any Catahoula left outside on its own is simply a problem in the making in one way or another, even if you have a securely fenced yard or have chained your Catahoula.

If, for whatever reason, your Catahoula will be spending time outside without a human presence, there are some things that you can do to minimize, if not eliminate, digging. I have driven past yards where dogs were simply left out on their own, and if this will be the case with your Catahoula, digging can be eliminated or controlled in a number of ways.

1. Make an area where your Catahoula will be allowed to dig to its heart's content. Use stones or a few sticks to mark out the perimeter and then bury some treats or toys in the spot. You will have to monitor your Catahoula until it has

become accustomed to using this area, and leading your Catahoula to the designated area and praising it when digging is done there can help to prevent your yard from becoming an obstacle course and moonscape. Over the course of time, the earth at the designated spot may become thinned out so be sure to add new material when necessary.

2. Exercise can often eliminate the digging problem. Taking your Catahoula on a daily walk (as long as it isn't too hot) and playing with it can help to drain off some of that excess energy and leave your Catahoula too tired to dig.

3. Spending time teaching your Catahoula some tricks can help it feel like it's doing something constructive as well as getting some attention from you.

While digging is not the worst behavior a Catahoula can engage in, it certainly can be annoying and can destroy your yard if your Catahoula is an especially vigorous digger and you leave it outside unsupervised. The best approach is to analyze why your Catahoula is doing it and then find a workable solution – even if this means keeping your Catahoula inside with you.

Chewing

Although puppies are undoubtedly the worst when it comes to inappropriate chewing, dogs of any age can cause destruction to your home and belongings. When the 'baby teeth' of puppies begin to break through the gums, and several months later when the adult teeth do so, the pup will have an instinctive drive to chew to relieve the discomfort and help the teeth emerge by chewing on anything it can reach. You may be surprised at how much damage a small puppy can do when teething. Our puppies, weighing only a couple of pounds, acted like beavers on our wooden dining room chairs. Yes, we gave them chew hooves and toys, but they preferred furniture (they could sometimes be distracted by squeaky toys). We directed them away from the chair legs, but they were persistent and rather cunning and did manage to do some pretty respectable damage to them. However, as soon as the teeth were through, they stopped chewing immediately and have never set tooth to furniture, clothing, or shoes in the following 11 years. We were philosophical about it, tried preventing it as much as possible, and shrugged off the damage.

Puppies, like human babies, also use the mouth as an exploratory tool, and tend to put anything they can between their teeth. A Catahoula puppy, after giving a new object a close sniff, will probably grab it with its mouth. Your pup has no concept of the value of any object in your home; everything is simply a potential chew.

However, although most puppy chewing is the result of teething, you should take your puppy to the vet when this behavior begins, to make sure that there isn't a nutritional problem present as well. An upset of the stomach and/or intestinal tract can also cause a puppy (or dog) to chew. Worms can also cause this behavior, so make sure that these are ruled out also.

Most parents discover that the easiest way to get through their toddler's exploratory phase is to 'child-proof' the home. This works well with Catahoula puppies, too, and it's probably a good idea to 'puppy-proof' your home when you bring a young dog into it. Removing or protecting objects that might be destroyed or cause harm to the puppy will protect the pup and keep you from getting angry and frustrated: it's a good idea to cover electric cords and remove valuable pieces of furniture until the puppy grows out of its chewing phase.

Giving your puppy something else to chew on can work with some pups, but from my own experience, it will not work every time. Always monitor your Catahoula puppy when it is chewing, even if this involves an 'approved' chew. Some puppies have much stronger jaws than you might imagine (ours did) and not only were they able to chew through chair legs, they were also able to completely pull apart toys to get at the squeaker. You should never leave your Catahoula puppy or dog alone with a rawhide chew – it's easy for the dog to chew off a piece and swallow it raising the possibility of an intestinal obstruction or choking.

Once the teething stage is over, most puppies will abandon the worst of their chewing behavior. All dogs love to chew to some extent, but dogs that continue destructive chewing after teething are indicating that a larger problem exists.

1. Catahoulas with separation anxiety often exhibit destructive chewing. Until the basic problem is resolved (see above) the dog will continue to chew and destroy.

2. Dogs that are not receiving the proper amount of exercise are more likely to expend some of their spare energy by chewing. Make sure that you give your chewing Catahoula a long walk every day (except when it's too hot), and take the time to play with it, too; Catahoulas that are tired and have worked out their energy will be less likely to chew inappropriately.

3. Dogs that are bored will simply chew for something to do. Even a dog whose main reason in life is to be a companion will become bored without some kind of stimulation. In addition to providing enough exercise, teach your Catahoula tricks or engage in new games with it; this will help to keep your Catahoula mentally engaged.

4. Stressed Catahoulas will chew just to relieve some of the tension. An uncomfortable home situation or a new pet or even a new baby can cause stress. Helping your Catahoula

124

become used to the new family member can help relieve the chewing problem, and maintaining a calmer atmosphere in the home will also help. Catahoulas are very sensitive to human moods and behavior.

Hopefully, it is needless to say that physical punishment and shouting have no place in correcting destructive chewing. Reinforce positively when your puppy or dog is chewing something it should. If you catch the animal chewing up the furniture or an article of clothing, pull it away, or remove the object from your Catahoula. You can say "No" once to your Catahoula, but don't yell or repeat the command. If the problem persists, consider using an animal behaviorist.

Jumping Up

Few people enjoy being jumped upon by their dog or by anybody else's. Children can be knocked over by dogs jumping on them and this can even be a problem for adults depending on the size of the dog. However, it will still be viewed as an annoyance by most people when a dog jumps up on them.

Jumping develops from the Catahoula puppy or dog's natural greeting behavior. Dogs greet one another by sniffing the other's face, and when puppies or dogs jump up they are simply trying to do the same thing – get close to our faces. Most of us inadvertently reinforce jumping when the Catahoula is a cute puppy and it jumps up to say hello when we have returned from being away.

Almost universally, the usually suggested methods to be used to curb the jumping habit all have a whiff of the Medieval about them: spray the dog in the face with water, step on the dog's feet, knee the dog in the chest, wrestle it to the ground by stepping on its leash, or even hurt the dog's forefeet by squeezing them hard. When you think about it, isn't this just a bit draconian for a Catahoula that is just happy to see you?

The most sensible thing of course, is to curb jumping while your Catahoula is still a puppy and before the behavior pattern has become ingrained. Preventing jumping behavior will go hand in hand with obedience training. The best approach is to use the "Sit" and "Stay" commands for the puppy when you or anyone else comes into the home. It's also a good idea to train the pup to go to a specific place when you come in, such as next to a chair or on its bed. This will take some time as you are going to have to overcome some instinctive behavior (especially if you have already been allowing your puppy to jump up). Rely on positive reinforcement and treats to help teach your puppy to greet you more calmly and without jumping up. Once the pup is restraining itself, kneel in front of it to let it access your face and greet it affectionately.

You will have to repeat this over and over until your Catahoula puppy or dog learns to connect sitting and waiting to be greeted with rewards such as affection and treats. As with other training, repeat the lesson several times over the course of the day, going in and out, to accustom your dog to the new behavior you require. Don't overdo it to the extent that either of you become bored or frustrated.

When you see your Catahoula puppy or dog getting ready to jump up onto you, step aside or turn your body so that your Catahoula misses. This should be taught in conjunction with the "Sit" and "Stay" commands. If you do come in and your Catahoula refrains from jumping, make sure to praise it, even if it isn't in the 'right spot' and isn't sitting. A small step is better than none.

Some measure of success can also be achieved if you use a toy as a distraction. Before your Catahoula pup or dog reaches you, offer the toy. This will usually redirect your Catahoula's attention from you and prevent jumping.

Territorial Marking

Male Catahoulas are not the only ones that will engage in territorial marking in the home – females will, too, under specific circumstances. We found that our female Catahoulas would mark territorially when they first came into the house, and also when they returned from a stay in the veterinary hospital. This was deliberate on their part but was not repeated; they evidently felt the need to either establish or re-establish their presence in the home and we ignored it completely. A one-off marking can likely be totally ignored; it's when the problem is ongoing that steps will have to be taken to curb it.

There are a handful of reasons why Catahoulas, usually male, will use urine to stake out their territory. A trip to the vet should be taken to rule out any medical problems, but generally, territorial urine marking has other reasons. Catahoulas that have not been neutered will also be more prone to this problem behavior than those that have been.

1. A worst case scenario is when your Catahoula feels that it is the dominant member of the household – the alpha. Male dogs that do this will often keep their human charges in line with growling or nips, so the marking is just a manifestation of a badly out-of-control situation in the first place. Keep in mind that your male Catahoula has the same instincts as any other type of dog breed, and it will try to lord it over you if you allow it.

2. Catahoulas of either gender will often mark when a new pet is introduced into the household, they evidently feel the need to establish themselves as 'top dog' immediately and let the newcomer know its place.

3. A new family member, such as a new baby or spouse, often prompts some territorial marking. Whether this is done to establish peck order or simply from stress is not known, and this usually occurs only once.

4. A Catahoula that is under stress or suffering from separation anxiety will be much more likely to mark the home. This kind of marking can be repeated, so finding the underlying cause and addressing it is vital.

Curing territorial marking in the home can be difficult, especially if the Catahoula is acting from a position of superiority over the humans. In this case, a way must be found to restore the normal 'pecking order' in the home. This is best done by obedience training, which will help to teach your Catahoula how to behave and to respond to your signals. Catahoulas that persistently urine mark in the home to demonstrate their status over their humans will often also show resource guarding aggression to the humans as well – the dog will growl, snarl, or bark when someone attempts to sit on a couch that the Catahoula believes is its personal property.

If the Catahoula is not marking to show its superiority, the owner should try to analyze why the animal is doing so, especially if this behavior appears suddenly. Accustoming your Catahoula to a new pet or family member can take some time, but most Catahoulas will come round fairly quickly if they are rewarded with treats and praise when acting appropriately towards the new member.

Clean up the urine immediately to remove a stimulus to future marking. You will need to use not only soap and water, but an enzyme cleaner to remove the odor completely. Enzyme cleaners will break down the organic components that soap cannot. Several applications may be needed before the smell is gone. Never use ammonia or a cleaner that contains ammonia – ammonia is a major component of urine and this will only intensify the attraction.

Keeping a close eye on your Catahoula and when it starts to show signs that it's getting ready to urinate, hustle it outside. Once it has urinated appropriately, be sure to positively reinforce this behavior by praising your Catahoula and giving it a treat.

Catahoulas that must be left alone for a part of the day will be more difficult to handle in regards to urine marking. Sometimes this can be done by keeping your Catahoula in a particular area; part of a room can be partitioned off, or a crate might be employed. However, any dog will urinate if they are not given the opportunity to do so every few hours, and a dog that has finally urinated after being left alone for 7 or 8 hours is certainly not responsible for this; this is not territorial marking, just desperation. If you are unable to walk your Catahoula during the day, please consider having a relative, neighbor, or pet sitter give your Catahoula a chance to relieve itself outside.

Punishment for urine marking is never called for and will only serve to make your Catahoula fearful and possibly aggressive. Territorial marking can be difficult to correct, and in extreme cases, your veterinarian could prescribe medication to help curb the behavior. A trip to the vet should be one of your first steps, to rule out any medical problems.

Chapter Nine: Conclusion

Positive Reinforcement

Positive reinforcement involves using nothing but praise when your Catahoula does something correctly, but ignoring undesirable behavior. This training method is probably the only one that should be used for any kind of basic training: obedience, crate, agility, hunting, etc. Rewarding a Catahoula puppy or dog for doing the right thing generally has long lasting results and provides a training structure that the Catahoula will be less likely to break.

While this is the most appropriate training method when serious behavior problems are not involved, it will also take longer than the old 'thumbscrew' methods to achieve results. Multiple repetitions will have to be made to teach your pup the correct way to behave, and a good deal of patience and forbearance will be required. However, the results are generally long lasting and will produce a confident Catahoula that will be a joy to be around.

Positive reinforcement can also be used to correct what might be considered more 'minor' behavior problems such as soiling the house and barking. These are annoyances and pose no real physical threat to people, so can be dealt with by using patience, praise, and treats. Biting, growling, snarling, and other dominance issues may be too serious, and require immediate correction, to use positive reinforcement exclusively. And, while proponents of positive reinforcement deny that they are trying to be 'pack leaders' or are using any kind of dominance when correcting problem behavior, the fact that the offending dog will be taken to the basement for a period of time, or confined to a crate is showing that the human is the pack leader – he or she is directly controlling the dog's behavior. It is fine that no physical violence was carried out on the dog, but the dog has still been put into a subordinate position where it has to do what the human decides. This is certainly not wrong, but the human has become the pack leader and is telling the underling what to do.

Pack-Leader (Alpha) Training

This has been the basic and most widely used training approach until fairly recently. This system teaches the dog that it is always – always – subordinate to every human being in the house, and has been applied with various levels of correction. On the one hand, according to this theory, you will have some physical correction, such as an alpha roll or slamming the dog to the ground, when the dog has exhibited poor behavior. This is obviously completely inappropriate for house soiling or other non-violent infractions, but is often used when the dog has posed a physical threat to someone in the home.

However, correction collars such as shock collars, choke collars, and prong collars are also not the solution to training, even when there is a serious behavioral problem. Physically punishing a dog is also obviously wrong and abusive, too, and will be more likely to produce more behavioral problems.

Some trainers still use the alpha roll to correct serious behavior problems, but extreme care should always be exercised if you decide to use this yourself. There have been problems such as the dog attacking the person rolling it, or serious damage done to the dog, so any aggression issues should be discussed with your veterinarian. However, as these biting problems usually grow from behavior that was not corrected when the dog was a puppy, the best answer is probably to let the puppy know that growling, snarling, and biting will not be tolerated the first time that the pup exhibits this. A stern "No!" will often be sufficient to let your errant Catahoula puppy understand that certain behavior is not allowed; this will not scar the puppy for life.

Many behavior problems arise because the Catahoula puppy, and then the adult dog, simply does not understand its position in the household hierarchy. And while early wolf studies were definitely flawed as they were based on captive wolves in a zoo, watching a video or reading about wild wolf behavior will highlight that there are definitely wolves that are in charge and wolves that are not.

The wolves that are not in charge are nipped, growled at, and threatened when they overstep what the pack leaders consider to be their boundaries. Yes, the pack leaders are the parents, but they also are the arbiters of pack life; humans behave this way, too, if they want a peaceful home life – unless an adult rules the roost, family life is chaos. Life in a wolf pack is not a slice of the peaceable kingdom, despite the fiction promulgated in Farley Mowat's book "Never Cry Wolf". Consider that Mowat promulgated that wolves lived almost exclusively on mice and other small game, rather than pulling down deer, moose, and anything else they can get their teeth into, and then ask yourself why this person is considered to be some kind of arbiter of canine behavior.

Some people who believe completely in positive reinforcement object to even using the word "No". I agree it should be avoided as much as possible, but no dog is going to be permanently scarred if its owner says "No" or "Stop" during the training process. Dogs, even Catahoulas, are rubbery and resilient and will respect and love you more if you and the other household humans are in the alpha position.

Alpha training fell into disrepute for several reasons: some trainers evidently confused training with torture, and trainers promoting positive reinforcement felt it necessary to completely discard the 'old' training method.

A Balanced Approach

Perhaps the best way to approach dog training is to use a combination of positive reinforcement and pack leader training, with a heavy emphasis on the positive. Despite what some trainers now say, it **is** important for the humans in the household to be at the top of the peck order, and correcting inappropriate behavior in a Catahoula puppy, using mostly positive reinforcement for good behavior, but letting the pup know when it has done something very bad, such as biting, with a loud reprimand or even a poke to the shoulder, will often nip this kind of behavior in the bud, before it becomes a real part of the animal's psychological make-up – the longer that problems are allowed to exist, the more difficult they will be to correct. However, never should correction become abuse; if you are unable to correct a problem quickly and without using excessive force, you must seek the help of an animal behaviorist.

Oddly enough, using positive reinforcement exclusively can cause the development of problems just as much as can an emphasis on negative reinforcement; dogs who were subjected to constant negative stress were 25% more likely to become aggressive, but the flip side is that most dogs that received only positive reinforcement developed behavior problems at a higher rate than dogs that received either verbal or physical corrections. In fact, positive reinforcement, when not used in conjunction with some negative, made the dogs more aggressive and fearful – could it be that the dogs felt insecure because there was no real leader? Being in authority does not mean that punishments are distributed constantly, but rather that someone is overseeing (wisely, we hope) the behavior of all individuals in the household and is helping to keep everything on an even keel.

When training your new Catahoula puppy, definitely rely on positive reinforcement for most of the process, but combine it with some 'soft' negatives when needed. Catahoulas are intelligent, and at some level seem to understand that they are not intended to be the leader of a human pack. Submission to the owners does not mean that the Catahoula has to cringe and approach the humans on its belly. It just means that the dog knows it can rely on the humans to run the household and that its place is safe and secure.

Made in the USA
Middletown, DE
29 December 2015